PARIS IN THE TWENTIES

TEXT BY ARMAND LANOUX

PARIS
IN THE TWENTIES

GOLDEN GRIFFIN BOOKS / ESSENTIAL ENCYCLOPEDIA

ARTS, INC., 667 Madison Avenue, New York, 21, N. Y.

TRANSLATED BY E. S. SELDON

© 1960 by Robert Delpire, éditeur

Published in the United States of America by
Arts, Inc. All rights reserved.
Library of Congress Catalog Card Number
59-12382. Printed in France.

When I look back over those ten years,
it seems always to have been the Fourteenth of July.
The tricolor was always flying.

Maurice Sachs

Paul Morand put the last touches to his essay entitled " 1900 " in December, 1930. One of the leading spirits of the epoch just closing, he made the fatal mistake of looking back nostalgically. If, like Lot's wife, he was promptly turned into a pillar of salt, we may be sure it was no ordinary salt, but salt of a peculiarly Twenties variety—which went by the trade name Rodell, and was used for soaking feet tired and sore from dancing the Charleston. The same dreadful fate lies in store for us all.

Thirty years had passed between Morand's witty piece and the period he tried to describe. Thirty years is about the right distance for the literary photographer to keep between himself and his subject. Only a few more than that stand between us and the mid-Twenties. An optical illusion that comes from having lived through them makes the Twenties seem to have passed more quickly than any years before. And yet, quickly or slowly, all the years slip by.

It was only yesterday—during the years just after World War II, for instance—that references to the Nineteen Twenties aroused no more than contemptuous smiles. Now, all of a sudden, we feel more tenderly toward the period. Good, bad, or indifferent, it was what it was. Josephine Baker, the first phonograph records, " La Violettera," Damia, Rudolf Valentino, the costumes and styles of decoration of the Twenties—they are all making their comeback these days, on stage and screen and in our personal mythologies of the recent past. The public went wild over a revival of the 1923 *L'Ecole des Cocottes*, in

" They have a soul, the roses, for they are women, roses." Drawing by A.-E. Marty. Hat by Marthe Collot.

which the actresses wore short-skirted chemises in gold and silver lamé, and it is once again humming the *Danseur de Charleston*. Young ladies are discovering the make-up trick their mothers could have told them about all along: that smudge under the eye. And Van Dongen, whose models and costumes suddenly strike us as ageless, is finding his pictures worth more than ever before.

" We slid down the hill to 1939 the same way the period of the Nineties slid down to 1914," Paul Morand wrote in 1941, and added, " We sank into the abyss as into some kind of pleasure." Today we have no idea where we are heading, either, but the fact that we are not so gay about it may not be very important, in the end. Morand, who portrayed the Twenties in such books as *Ouvert la Nuit* and *L'Europe Galante*, gave the period one of its characteristic styles of life. If today it is the turn of the model society he created to become model in another sense, and sit for its portrait, it is hard to say who should be pitied more: they or we.

Paris 1925

The French title of this book is *Paris 1925*, because we French do not, like the Anglo-Saxons, think very much in terms of chronological decades. Instead of saying (what is not impossible, but awkward in French) " the Twenties " or " the Nineties," we say " 1925 " or " 1900 "—i.e., we let a date midway in a sequence of years denote the few years before and after that constitute a minor epoch. Thus, to us " 1900 " arbitrarily denotes a period extending from the Dreyfus Case to the First World War. Similarly, " 1925 " denotes the ten years extending from the

end of World War I to the world-wide crisis of 1929. This style of expression makes us stress mid-epoch phenomena, as when we note that there was in Paris in 1925 a public exhibition as typical of the Twenties as the *Exposition Universelle* (or World's Fair) of 1900 was of its period. 1925 was the year of the *Exposition des Arts Décoratifs*, promptly abbreviated to *Arts Décos*. To contemporaries it was a revelation and a revolution in taste: nothing would ever again be quite the same. With this event the Twenties styles of decoration and design were set in their characteristic molds. If, generically, they were aptly summed up in the formula *Amours, Délices et Orgues* (Loves, Thrills, and Organ Music). The fabulously luxurious houseboats which the great couturier Paul Poiret had built and decorated for his use, provide a typical instance. Actually, in retrospect, a good deal of Twenties design seems less brand new than a logical development from what the French call (in English) "modern style," and the Anglo-Saxons (in French) "*Art Nouveau.*" From 1900, in short.

Although for his own reasons Maurice Sachs dated his book *La Décade de l'Illusion* 1922-1932, he was describing the same period we call *Paris 1925*. The fateful years: good, bad, or indifferent... They start before and continue after *1925*.

Between Two Holocausts

Some thirty years later, the Twenties are for me a crisscrossing street crowd of memories,

" *It is ridiculous, even impossible, to try to get about Paris and get one's business done with a 40 h. p. car.*" *Place de l'Opéra.*

9

among which stand out the women's dresses, severely geometrical with enormous printed flowers, or with gold and silver threads worked into the fabric, or beaded... heavily beaded.

Poster by Cassandre.

But there was also *L'Enfant Roi* in weekly installments—Continued in Our Next—which I read in my suburban *Kursaal.* My first intimations of the glories of Montparnasse reached me through drawings I saw in the shop run by an old man named Canard in the Rue Notre-Dame-des-Champs (on the other side of the Seine). He sold painters' supplies and busts of the philosopher Seneca. Surely it was only a step from here to a world where people wore masks, where the Barbarian Horde periodically swept down, where something called the Quat'z' Arts took place annually, and where the wine ran redder than blood...

Those were the days when self-styled " revolutionaries of the word " brandishing paper-bound volumes, enlisted their shock troops under the banner of Modern Literature and Modern Painting and plotted their offensives in obscure cafés, some *Boîte à Joujoux* (Box of Toys) or *Petite Chaumière* (Cozy Cottage)... Those were the days when youth was everywhere in revolt against its elders, perhaps most truly desperate in its anxiety to appear so. The future parents of today's hot-rod racers and juvenile delinquents...

Looking back, I can still smell the ink of those manifestoes, just off the press, and recall the magic of those nights when Léon-Paul Fargue, cruising around Paris in his G. 7, would end up at the *Lipp*, driven aground by the exhaustion of a not inexhaustible allowance from his family. I can remember wandering as a child of twelve among the crowds at the exhibition of the *Arts Décos,* at once fascinated and secretly repelled... and the cellar club in the Rue Blomet, favorite haunt of Negroes in Paris, then taken up by the poet Robert Desnos as, twenty years later, it would be taken up by Jean-Paul Sartre... And as soon as I was a very few years older, I fell under the spell of those more considerable wonders of the Twenties, identifiable under such names as Gide, Cendrars, Mac Orlan, Proust, Valéry, Breton, Cocteau...

Of course, there was much about the Twenties that was dubious, as well as much that was admirable. A bit of a sickroom smell—but also a good deal of genuine revolt. If the emphasis upon the gynecological, the genito-urinary, was a little ridiculous, there was also profound respect for individual liberty. Less attractive were such phenomena as a phony Bohemianism which made

The Boulevards in the Twenties.

Mannequins Display the Fall Styles.

it possible for future tycoons and politicians to pose as struggling young artists and writers; a phony kind of political passion which never got beyond arguments at sidewalk cafés; the apotheosis of the superb Amedeo Modigliani, by the very persons who had driven him to his early grave in Père Lachaise, and had most profited from his death. It is not pleasant to think of him, soon to be honored by all the world as Lord of Leghorn, driven to the wall by his most slavish courtiers...

Those were the days of expensive limited editions (sometimes bibliographically falsified), when the tango reigned supreme, the last days of the great Ballets Russes (whose embalmed corpse survives to this day in the ballet productions of the Paris Opéra), the days when the music of Honegger and Milhaud burst upon our ears—" Have you heard Milhaud's score for *Le Bœuf sur le Toit?* "—and the great days of Nijinsky—" Have you ever seen such prodigious leaps? "—days when the dour Mauriac was casting envious eyes at the ferment of Surrealist activity, when Maritain was inspiring a number of illustrious conver-

Van Dongen's Psychoanalysis of the Woman of the Twenties.

sions to Catholicism and when Max Jacob was heard to pronounce: " God loathes Cocteau," and the great days of Cocteau himself (today still capitalizing, at the Académie and in the pages of *Paris-Match*, on the enfant terrible he then was), the days of Josephine Baker's rise to celebrity and of Coty's (the megalomaniac manufacturer of perfume) to notoriety, when other names on everyone's lips included the glib-tongued Merle (the confidence man), the bearded dressmaker Poiret, Mahatma Gandhi, Sigmund Freud, and Voronov, and when the most popular novelists were Pierre Frondaie and Maurice Dekobra. What a bouillabaisse they make, when we throw all these fish from the Seine into the same pot !

The Twenties thought and spoke of themselves as " post-war." In French it was even possible to speak of *the* post-war, a name for the epoch. Subsequent events like the evacuation from Dunkerque and the breakthrough at Sedan oblige us to look for a more modest characterization. Now and forever after, the Nineteen Twenties are to be thought of as one long, wild, lavish party, elaborate if not always elegant, a gala celebration between two world-wide disasters.

Myths of the Twenties (Clearance Sale)

First, we have the blue-eyed blond sailor and his girl: his ship is in port for a few hours or a few days, and he has a woman in every port. Pierre Mac Orlan, the adventurer who stayed at home and wrote, and Alain Gerbault, the adventurer who went to the ends of the earth and never said a word about his adventures, were the sources of this myth. In the liter-

At the Arts Décos.

15

The Bois de Boulogne: Family Aspect, by Charles Laborde.

ature of the epoch, dockside farewells, tales of sailors and sirens, of soldiers in the Foreign Legion and deserters from it—travelers all—are recounted to the sad-happy lilt of a single accordion playing on shipboard, in barracks, or down a dingy sidestreet in some harbor city.

Capital I for Insecurity; capital A for Adventure.

Next we have the severe symbols of Cubism: the guitar, the imitation wood panel, the pack of cigarettes, the clay pipe—all of them treated much more airily, much less seriously, than at first seems. Over here are the metaphysical dummies of Giorgio de Chirico, the painter who denounced his own genius. For sale to settle an estate: display articles from the windows of pharmaceutical supply houses, artificial limbs, and other trappings of literary naturalism.

And here are the scenery and props from all those *Olympiques* (from Paul Morand to Montherlant): parading athletes, stadiums, chronometers, shower baths, and sun-tan lotions. Here, too, the night club, the open-cockpit plane, the Dôme and the Coupole, the villa in the South of France, the Negro playing the saxophone, and the English sergeant-major (female) guarding the virtue of her troop of English chorus girls.

Here are the weighty tomes of the psycho-analysts and the treatises on relativity. They seem the most worthwhile today. And here are the false passports, the official papers granting special privileges to the already privileged, Cosmopolitanism, panegyrics to the Machine, the de luxe international trains so beloved of Valéry Larbaud, Abel Gance's *La Roue*, Dekobra's *La Madone des Sleepings* (" The Madonna of the Pullmans "), and Frondaie's cult of elegance, the Hispano-Suiza.

Over here in a group are a Harlequin, a playing card, and a rooster by Picasso, and Max Jacob's leather dice cup. Here is a plaster cast of Cocteau's hands, Philippe Soupault's book on Lautréamont, the songs that Damia and Yvonne Georges sang, rare numbers of the review *La Sirène*. Here is Blaise Cendrars' amputated hand, and one of Francis Carco's daggers for street-fighting, the " switchblade " of the period. And the old thriller *Fantômas*, as Robert Desnos revised it.

The Bois de Boulogne: The Races.

Here are faded copies of long-dead literary and art reviews, today worth their weight, if not in gold, then in gold paper: *Sic, Nord-Sud, Messages, Bifin, Le Grand Jeu*, etc.

And finally we come to the Public Enemy Number One, the gangster, and the beautiful dancer who is really a spy. Here are the truly popular novels in which, despite the rise of the automobile age, despite mass- and over-production, murder was still being committed in formal dress, including opera cloak and hat, and revolvers were always equipped with silencers... in which the bride was always being carried off by a drunken boor on her wedding night, to be restored to the bridegroom in the end, tearful but still intact... *Fantômas* dates back to 1913, but its greatest success came in the Twenties. It was the only period instance when popular taste was in agreement with that of the intellectuals.

Tattooed Roses

From her shoulders to below her hips, the woman of the Twenties was a rectangle. From waist to knees, she was a trapeze, narrower below than above. Her hair was worn short and straight, exposing at the back a hairline clipped and shaved. Her ears were weighted down with enormous earrings of imitation stones. Most of her crowning glory was hidden by a tight cloche hat, from which a single lock of hair was allowed to peep out, over the left eyebrow.

The over-all effect was nothing if not equivocal. What it seemed to say was, " I'm just a little girl." A second pair of lips was superimposed upon the first, of another shape.

Love and Gasoline: Suzy Vernon at the Wheel.

One lipstick of the period was named " The Eternal Wound." Bracelets around the wrists and neck seemed to mock at the durability and singleness of attachments, to emphasize the fragility of all ties. Seen in profile, the woman of the Twenties was a windblown angel; face to face, she was a robber of graves, a vampire, her mouth blood-red.

As late as 1924, skirts came no higher than mid-calf. It was in 1925 that women were wholly liberated below the waist. Their legs suddenly acquired a life of their own, for the first time appearing to be organs grafted onto androgynous bodies, rather than subordinate parts of an organic femininity. Women now crossed their legs at any angle, and in view of the increased exposure took pains to enhance the beauty, the smoothness, and the lines of their lower limbs as never before. Depilatoried and pumiced, variously made up and decorated—with ankle bracelets, with garters, with tattooed roses—all this leg-consciousness only further emphasized the highly artificial modesty encasing the body above them—most notably, a bust imperceptible enough to make a new-born baby howl. (In any case, children were put out to nurse.) As Mistinguett danced, she sang:

> They say I've lovely gams,
> And what they say is true !

In spite of all these developments, which spread rapidly and widely, *La Gazette du Bon Ton* and the more specialized fashion magazines kept right on talking in terms of

◄ *Avenue des Acacias: Twenties Foreground, Nineties Background.*

Bois de Boulogne: Another View, by Vertès. ►

an " eternal feminine ".as though no profound revolution had occurred : " Strange, unreal in its perverse charm, this gown called 'Reptile' is in sinuous velvet, striped and speckled like the skin of the boa constrictor. Only Poiret could have brought off something like this, additional proof, were any needed, that Poiret stops at nothing."

Nonetheless, the *chansonniers* were making observations like these:

Every day the women of today
Are up to new and better tricks.
They even play the banjo now,
Drink cocktails, drive their own cars.
Oh, me ! Oh, my !
Well, now they're going themselves one better :
It wasn't enough to cut off their hair,
Now they're letting us see their calves
And even higher, all the way up !

From 1922 on, the creations of the great dressmakers (among whom the men became the best known) began to be given titles like these: " When One Loves, " " Waiting for Him, " " Snuggle-Up Time, " " Kiss Me " (this in English), " First Encounter, " " Five to Seven, " " Will He Come? " For all the flashiness of the period, many of its costumes were expressive of a wide-eyed innocence—deceptive, in that the gowns so designated were purchased to be worn at house parties in the country where morals could be extremely free.

The emancipated woman of the Twenties presents the silhouette of the period. Paul Poiret, at the close of his long career, dressed her up so that Kisling, not long after, might undress her, and in order that Van Dongen, a more moralistic painter, might consign her to the grave in a little raspberry and lime-green ensemble.

Waiting for the Last Judgment

About the time they were singing " *Pas sur la bouche, ça m'effarouche* " (Not on the mouth—it scares me there), women were wearing flimsy underclothes with crossword puzzles printed on them. Maud Loti had a portrait of herself embroidered over her heart and became famous for saying " Shit " in public. This was the period when apartments began to fill up with dolls, extra cushions, and lucky charms: an essentially childish femininity striking back against being tied down. This was the age of bric-à-brac, much of it brand new: Lalique glasses, drawings by Robj, ivory manicure sets, Japanese tea services, elaborate candy boxes, and incense burners.

Another craze of the pre-World War I days was revived: the ladybug motif in jewelry and decoration. Again, the *chansonniers* did not let this go by unnoticed and wrote a song for Estelle, who added ladybugs to her collection of personal fetishes.

And at the same time that this ladybug craze was going strong, the vogue for the *tom-pouce* (Tom Thumb), a short umbrella, was at its height. To go anywhere without one of these was to be caught without one's totem, to be lacking a secondary sexual characteristic.

The fashionable word wherever fashion was concerned, was *le chic*. " What is Chic? " was a popular question asked by reporters of society figures at this time. When Princesse Lucien Murat was asked this question in the old *Intransigeant* (a newspaper which did not survive World War II), she made it seem the

Bois de Boulogne: The Heroines of Frondaie and Dekobra.

Bois de Boulogne: Outing in the Country.

prerogative of the very poor. " Chic," she said, " requires nothing at all. It is much more the way you carry your head than the way you wear your clothes." All the same, the lady quoted was dressed by Poiret and Schiaparelli.

Marie Laurencin, the painter whom Apollinaire immortalized as Tristouze Ballerinette, had a different point of view. As she put it, " A woman is not a stick."

Kees Van Dongen, who was wearing a skullcap and a Japanese dressing gown when interviewed, muttered to the press that " Some women are chic in the very cheapest

dresses (well, at least 150 francs), while others who pay four or five thousand francs look a mess."

These figures need converting. The " threepenny franc " (as it was called after Poincaré's so-called stabilization) was worth fifty of today's francs. This means that " the very cheapest dresses " of which Van Dongen spoke would cost about 7,500 francs (about $21) today, and the 4,000 francs couturier gown would come to 200,000 francs (about $570) !

Engraving by Vertès.

24

Paul Poiret himself took exception to the so-called " cactus " silhouette, which Fernand Léger's paintings celebrate: " Up until now, women have been beautiful in an architectural sense, like a ship's prow. At the present time, they look like nothing so much as the undernourished boys you see working in post offices."

Antoine—the coiffeur—was one of the deities of the Twenties. He supervised his own advertising. " Artist of genius. Wields the scissors and comb like the sculptor's chisel, and with unusual personal gifts. Creates about him an atmosphere unlike any other. Does the hair of the most chic members of the French and English aristocracy."

In appearance, he looked like a pudgy Rudolf Valentino.

Estelle, the ladybug heroine, went so far as to wear garters with little watches in them. That these acquired something of the function of taximeters is attested by the following quatrain, taken from a postcard of the period in the collection of Anatole Jakovsky:

Would you like to know what time it is?
You'll find my watch down here
In a place that never gets very cold,
And that fashion decrees should be seen.

Gillette, the safety-razor blade manufacturer, began to place ads in women's magazines. The Armpit, a matter for scandal when so much as mentioned in the novels of the late nineteenth century, was shortly to be Shaved. Nothing less than a revolution in Cupid's domain—for the Nineties had been a hairy epoch. If things kept on taking this turn, Estelle would soon be shaving you-know-where, and *then* what would become of twenty centuries of Western eroticism?

Pierre Mac Orlan, the poet and novelist who quit Paris in the mid-Twenties for the leafy, faintly haunted environment of Saint-Cyr-sur-Morin, looked upon these developments with a prophetic eye. Writing about the drawings of Vertès, who had just been chosen to do the poster for the *Bal des Petits Lits Blancs* (the biggest society event of the Paris year, an annual hospital benefit), he observed: " The faces of the girls Vertès draws are pretty because they conform to what we see, to what we want to see in the women of this period. These lovely asexual creatures, glimpsed in passing, are marked with the classic sign of death. These groups forever on the move, alternately excited and overwhelmed by the rhythms of jazz, constitute a humanity made up of future victims."

Parade

Paris in the Twenties was the offspring of war, a war known at the time as The Great War. The stage was being set as early as 1917, when Cocteau launched one of the Twenties' passwords: *Parade*. He had volunteered for active service and had been accepted, after deceiving the medical authorities as to his state of health, and he strolled along the Boulevard Montparnasse in a helmet painted lavender. Word got around that the French Army was experimenting with a new headpiece ! It was one of several occasions when the military and civilian senses of the French word *parade*, hitherto quite distinct, were to be forced into new and richly ambiguous combinations.

Place Clichy. Painting by Bonnard.

Here, the reader must be reminded that the word *parade* has never conveyed in French one of its primary meanings in English. A " street parade " in French is not a *parade*, but a *défilé*, a *cortège*, or a *procession*. Besides its technical military senses (much the same in English as in French), its only other meaning was " ostentation " and its only link with entertainment one very limited usage among the folk who put on carnivals. The little show put on outside the tent or booth, to induce the public to step up and buy tickets for the main show or sideshow inside, was called a *parade*. It was this latter sense of the word that the Twenties was to expand and to bring into forced juxtaposition with the primary military senses. If a *parade des forains*—a sort of warming up, or come-on entertainment supplied by strolling players in a traveling carnival—was at the very opposite extreme from any full-dress military parade, it eventually became possible to combine the extremes and to speak, for example, of a *parade des morts*, meaning (for example) the sort of political exploitation and exhibitionism at the expense of the war dead, that attended the dedications of military cemeteries in France throughout the post-war years. The Paris which had improvised the defense of the Marne by taxicab was to reveal several more startling improvisations, not only of language.

While French soldiers had been acting out as best they could the un-Molièresque *Impromptu de Verdun*, dying like flies in the mud of the trenches, there had been mutinies at the front and the mutineers had been lined up and shot. Meanwhile, Paris became a city of soldiers invalided out, wealthy draft-dodgers, and old people, swelled by a constantly changing stream of men and officers on leave such as Colette wrote about (her " khaki and blue lieutenants " recalling that the color of the French uniform was changed in the course of the war). For company the troops on leave found young widows, and girls engaged in war work. All of them were driven underground to the cellars as the bombardments of Big Bertha became more and more accurate and the shells came closer and closer.

The terraces of cafés were jammed. Music halls and *caf'conc'* (cafés with orchestra) were so enormously popular that it was thought necessary officially to discount the gaiety. " If Paris seems still to smile, it is the forced smile of a France in pain."

Indeed, ladies' undergarments in the colors of the French flag were actually worn, and Mme Marthe Chenal, for one, was quite out of breath from singing the *Marseillaise* so often.

Meanwhile, most serious thought, much new poetry, and a number of painters soon to be famous, fled to the front, rather than behind the lines. As the shells kept falling and men kept dropping, it is remarkable, not that so many men were killed, but that even a few survived, who had kept on writing and sketching and reflecting seriously despite the knowledge that at any moment each might get the bullet or the shell with his name on it.

It was in this hectic atmosphere that the Twenties came to birth, obviously an " instrumental delivery." More than anything else, the new writing which shortly appeared both reflected the disorder and helped to encourage it. Boys still too young for college, let alone the Army, like Raymond Radiguet, used their own experiences—the

" Days and nights we drank it up, drank up our lives as through a straw." The Rotonde.

29

little ferryboats that run along the Marne, a love affair with the wife of a soldier at the front—to produce works quite as disturbing as those of their elder brothers in the trenches.

The devil *was* in the flesh, and the men capable of mounting a *Parade* or a *Mamelles de Tirésias* were ready in the wings. Even as the girls of the Boulevard Sébastopol were giving their last embraces to the victors of the Marne and the Yser (not to mention their last doses of syphilis and gonorrhea, for penicillin was as yet unknown), the echoes of the last bugle were being drowned out by the music of innumerable jazz bands.

Death of the Blue Lieutenant

Lt. Apollinaire was lying in bed. Around his forehead neatly arranged Velpeau bandages covered his wound:

A lovely Minerva is the offspring of my head
I am forever crowned with a bloody star.

It was November, 1918. The mild autumn weather coming in through the open window passed unnoticed by him, for the Spanish 'flu, the plague of 1918, had reopened his wound, and he had been asleep for two days, ever since the 9th.

Outside the windows the racketing of demobilized soldiers seemed to be spreading throughout the city, swelling gradually to the proportions of Armistice festivities as the streets filled with the harvest of the grapes of wrath: bugles blowing, whores and hysterics, sweethearts reunited, broken homes, an outpouring of frenzied humanity into the streets so enormous as nearly to dwarf Apollinaire's own funeral procession. While I reject as apocryphal the legend according to which the

crowd screamed " *A bas Guillaume!* " as he was laid to rest—" Down with Guillaume " meaning the poet rather than Wilhelm the Kaiser—still it is true that anything at all can happen on this planet. It is a legend with the Apollinaire touch, in any case.

And so he slept on, like a mummy. The bandages around his head while he was still alive prefigured the mummification that shortly followed in public opinion. If any one man may be said to have fathered the Paris of the Twenties, it was Apollinaire—who did not live to see his creation.

A new literary magazine devoted its first number entirely to him, and the names of the young contributors who proclaimed themselves his spiritual sons and brothers are noteworthy: Aragon, Cendrars, Cocteau, Dermée, Gonzague Fric, Max Jacob, Picabia, André Salmon, Tristan Tzara... And indeed these men did extend and continue Apollinaire's leads with respect to literature, art, and ideas. They prolonged Cubism, promoted Dada with notable success, and created Surrealism... They picked up, as it were, the torch of " pataphysics " which Apollinaire himself had had from the hands of the creator of *Ubu Roi*.

On June 24, 1917, at a theater in the Rue de l'Orient in Paris, the first performance of *Les Mamelles de Tirésias* was given. This was Apollinaire's burlesque defense of fecundity in wartime. The author himself had described the work as *surréaliste*, although at this time the first stammerings of Dada had scarcely spread beyond a small circle in Zürich, and what we think of today as Surrealism—meaning the Surrealist movement proper—would not be founded until 1924.

Nude, *by Gromaire.*

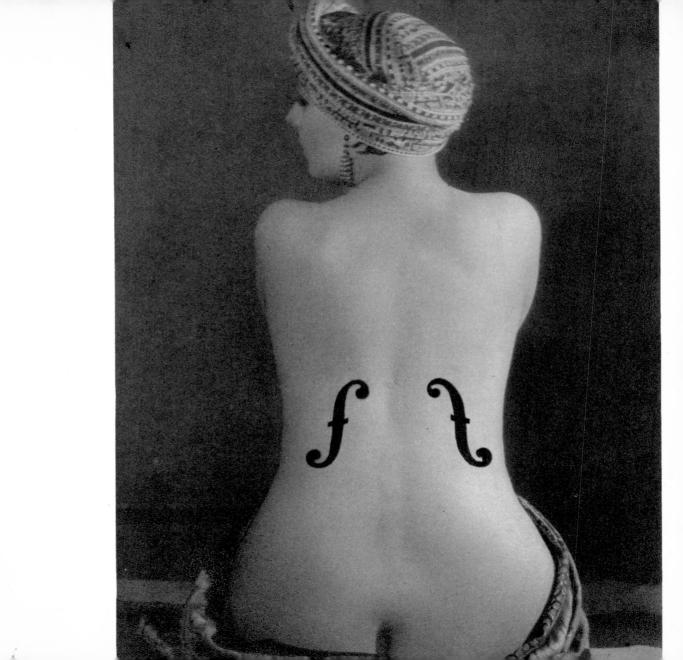

As Apollinaire explained, " I have forged the adjective 'surrealist'—the meaning of which is *not* ' symbolist' as M. Victor Basch claimed in his review of the play—so as to define as well as may be a tendency in art which, if not the newest thing under the sun, has never, at any rate, been used to formulate any credo, to advance any artistic or literary claim."

The play had been begun in 1903. As we look back today, we can see that there was more than one premonition of the Twenties in the intellectual and artistic climate at the turn of century. And at the same time we can recognize today that the Twenties were full of survivals of the Nineties and the pre-war years.

Jean the Bird-Catcher

Cocteau was the star, and he knew it better than anyone else. His signature was always " Jean "—followed by a crudely drawn star. His were the weaknesses of a star. His face, the way he combed his hair, his hands, all these personal details were fixed and unalterable in the public mind. He smoked opium. It was always public knowledge who his closest friends were, with whom he was currently linked. The star belongs to the public.

As Maurice Sachs, another glittering figure of the period, described it, " It was not at all unusual to find young people gathered outside wherever he lived, clustered around the door or even hanging from lampposts, in the chance of seeing him come in or go out. At night you were quite likely to stumble over

Kiki, by Man Ray. " *Kiki, don't look at me like that! You bother me!* "

them on the stairs—somehow they had got into the building and were sleeping stretched out on the steps. Like princes of another day, Cocteau held court. It was customary to call on him around eleven in the morning, and quite a company might be present as he arose and made his toilette."

His words in defense of Landru (the wife murderer whom Charlie Chaplin was to celebrate much later as Monsieur Verdoux) are as elegantly put together as they are disturbing. " The ordinary lover disposes of his memories by putting them on the fire: letters, gloves, flowers, locks of hair. Isn't it simpler to set fire to the lady herself? " A little crisscrossing of blue veins at the temples was the only clue to his secret weakness. He lived for his weaknesses, catered to them. He was gifted with ubiquity. His conversation, even enemies admitted, was a masterpiece. Memorable witticisms, striking word-pictures, acid observations—Cocteau's conversation was like a very elaborately designed fireworks display. And no question about its being designed: " I am a lie that always tells the truth."

Should we dismiss Cocteau as merely a literary equivalent to the acrobat Barbette? Most definitely not. An acrobat in the music hall of letters, certainly, but at the same time the very clearest mind, and the most acute; his advice was invariably sound. We must not blame him alone if the period could only envisage classicism in terms of clowns in dead white make-up. Moreover, Cocteau possessed a moral conscience. Running through the fun and games, the razzle-dazzle, are astonishing variations on the theme of the human condition, on " the difficulty of being." He was as devoted to his calling as circus people to theirs, conceiving of it the way others conceive of their religion.

The period needed a Wise Man cast in its own mold. Jean, who styled himself "The Bird-Catcher," was just that under his mask of frivolity.

The Devil in the Flesh

Max Jacob was one of the first to make Radiguet's acquaintance. "He was handsome and solemn. He seemed to have read everything. Nothing ruffled him. You saw him nearly every night at the *Bœuf sur le Toit*. He drank a good deal, but his expression never changed. He had rather thick lips and mulish eyebrows. His eyes were not incapable of a cruel gleam."

At fourteen this enfant terrible, who could also be a very good little boy, dazzled everyone with a book of poems to which he gave the wonderful title, *Les Joues en feu* (" Cheeks Aflame"). At the age of twenty, he was dead of typhoid fever. Into the intervening years he crowded a wealth of experience which would do credit to a septuagenarian, and he wrote *Le Bal du Comte d'Orgel* and *Le Diable au Corps*. Jean Cocteau said of him, "This boy not only taught us elegance, i.e. how the thunderbolt conceals its power, he also influenced us, giving us some of our profoundest leads."

Radiguet's short life took him no farther afield than from the suburban fastnesses of Parc Saint-Maur, served by a railroad with double-decker coaches for commuters, to Arcachon (a beach resort southwest of Bordeaux) where he spent his vacations, and from Montmartre to Montparnasse, the two poles of Paris' artistic and literary life. He came by his insurrectionary talents quite naturally: "Ever since 1789 they have been trying to make me think. Is it any wonder I have a headache?"

It is no secret any longer that the original of Marthe, the heroine of *The Devil in the Flesh*, was a schoolteacher in Saint-Maur. At least some portions of the plot actually transpired along the leafy banks of the Marne. A few years ago, Roland Dorgelès received a letter from a veteran of the 1914-18 war, one Gaston S..., the husband of that young schoolteacher. He had read *Le Diable au Corps*, and he was convinced that he and—more importantly—his wife (now dead) had been portrayed in it. "When you read this letter I shall have gone to be once more with the woman I loved, and who always loved me... One book, *Le Diable au Corps*, has ruined my life."

Gaston S... had married Alice while on leave. When the war was over and he came back the neighbors were not slow to inform him that during his absence his wife had given a good deal of special tutoring to a certain young scholar. Gaston S... managed not to believe the gossip until a day when the noted publisher Grasset, who was the first to go in for elaborate advertising in France, launched a book with the following blurb: "The masterpiece of the seventeen-year-old novelist Raymond Radiguet: LE DIABLE AU CORPS ".

As he read the book, with its powerful and convincing use of the first person singular, he became convinced that his wife had been the model for the character Marthe. Thirty years later, as she lay dying, he was still asking her to confirm or deny it. Her last words were, "I have never done anything to wrong you." Gaston S... is also dead. Who was telling the truth? The author, who meta-

Montparno's Blues. *Painting by Van Dongen.*

34

Van Dongen

morphosed a few events of his own experience into a novel, or one of its readers, who was so caught up in the narrative as to remain imprisoned in it?

Vavin: Crossroads of Montparnasse

When Cocteau returned to the scene in 1919, the custom had already grown up of using the *Salle Huyghens* in Montparnasse for recitals of new poetry. Always the coagulating agent in the bloodstream of his times, Cocteau began to sponsor new music as well. His intentions were no secret. He admitted himself, "Since these mysteries are beyond my ken, the least I can do is act as organizer for them." Kouski, the painter Kisling's dog, accompanied the works of the newest masters with an obbligato of howls. Pierre Bertin sang Georges Auric's *La Fête du Duc*. Erik Satie walked all the way from Arcueil-Cachan (a suburb on the other side of Paris) to be present. Others heard from were Darius Milhaud, Germaine Tailleferre, and Francis Poulenc. Now Cocteau, who sponsored these early concerts, was and remained an inhabitant of the Right Bank, not the Left. With his descents into Montparnasse he aroused more than ordinary interest in what was going on there. It was through his agency, at least in part, that what might have remained just another regional cultural activity rapidly became a Paris-wide and, eventually, an international phenomenon: a new school of French music.

Prior to 1914, when Montmartre was the center of literature and the arts, occasional sorties down to Montparnasse—visits to the

Department Store Christmas Decorations.

Les Sixdaymen: The Start of the Six-Day Bike Race in 1925.

country, as it were—had been made. You might have caught a glimpse of Apollinaire with his wife Jacqueline, a pretty redhead whom he nicknamed "Ruby," of Braque, or of Cendrars. Quite a number of foreign artists settled in Montparnasse in the immediate pre-war years, and during the war some of them served in the Foreign Legion. Gustave Coquiot was much too harsh when he described the Montparnasse of the early days in these terms: "Every nation in the world has exported its laziest males to Montpar-nasse, where they live piled together along the Boulevards Montparnasse and Raspail, in the Rue Campagne-Première, the Rue Delambre, the Rue de la Gaité, and the Rue d'Odessa."

Jean Giraudoux did a better job of explaining the attraction which Paris has for the foreigner: "The War of '14 was born out of the Germans' insensate desire to get to Montparnasse. Only, instead of coming one at a time by train, they tried to come all at once on foot."

Les Catherinettes: Annual Contest of Paris Shopgirls.

Flesh Pink, Strolling through the Bois

Pink was the dominant color of the Twenties, through the range of shades from Flesh to Coral, " from the wholesome shade of French Pink to the morbidity of Orchid and the ecclesiastical dignity of Cyclamen." It was the Pink Period. The artist Foujita appeared at a ball in Montparnasse wearing nothing much but some tattooing, and carrying a wicker cage inside which was Mme Foujita (Fernande Barrey), smiling and wearing a ribbon in her hair. On the cage was a neat sign bearing the words " Woman for Sale," followed by the letters " S. G. D. G." which signify in French " Not Guaranteed by the Government " (the phrase customary when a patent has been applied for and refused).

There was a great vogue for games of all sorts at this time: crossword puzzles, mah-

To the Greater Glory of Citroën: Style Gomina.

jongg, and innumerable card games. There was also a vogue for "tests." One of the most popular of these consisted of turning up a woman's handbag and describing her personality from the heterogeneous contents. Women were willing to play along with this sort of self-exposure. Should the revelations become too intimate, after all, they could always laugh at the amateur psychologist's discomfiture.

Meanwhile, survivors of the Nineties complained frequently and loudly of a steady lowering in the standards of public behavior. To the sing-song tune of *Nuits de Chine* (China Nights) the following cautionary words were sung:

> Since the dreadful war is over,
> All we see is
> Crimes, and children killing parents,
> Where will it end?
> Too many crimes
> Too many crimes
> Let's call a halt.
> Judges, get tough !
> Are we civilized, or are we not?

Victor Margueritte's novel *La Garçonne* sold 100,000 copies and created an enormous stir—as it seems today, for the wrong reasons. For *La Garçonne* was a typical 1900 novel, transposed into the mid-Twenties. Written in a coarsely naturalistic style, it was very like the novels of Georges Ohnet, but gingered up with sexy passages formerly considered unprintable. It did not, however, treat seriously the problem it claimed to deal with. Undeniably, the modern woman was becoming a *garçonne*—morally independent,

Georges Carpentier (in 1925) greets Jack Dempsey (who beat him in 1921).

" Some of these new models can do over sixty! "

competitive with men, " masculine " in certain respects—but Victor Margueritte's heroine became a *garçonne* only against her will, without really wanting to. What would have been much more valuable would have been an attempt to comprehend the genuinely emancipated woman of the era.

Nonetheless, the book aroused such a storm of discussion, and so many protests, that Victor Margueritte was stricken from the rolls of the Legion of Honor.

What was called *la surprise-party*—meaning almost any sort of impromptu gathering of acquaintances—had come into fashion as early as 1919. In social relations as in other connections, the general tendency was towards anarchy, towards " I-don't-give-a-damn-ism." In 1921 Willemetz wrote the theme song of this highly relaxed point of view:

> Don't let anything bother you
> It's a thing I never ever do
> Your little troubles
> Are only bubbles
> Everything is going to be all right !

At the same time, the Prefecture of Police was being obliged to patrol the Bois constantly, as never before in history. Not the Bois de Vincennes, that leafy retreat so popular with the Parisian masses, but the Bois de Boulogne,

41

almost the private park of the upper classes, adjacent to the most fashionable quarters of Paris. Obviously, the police must do something about it—but just what? For one thing, you could never be sure you weren't arresting somebody very important indeed. At the height of this curious vogue for sportive encounters in the Bois de Boulogne—a chapter in Paris social history today closed—the following popular song gave a few hints as to the nature of its appeal:

> It's the blasé ones
> Who go there now
> To restore their jaded senses.
> Just brushing against
> Couples in long embrace
> Revives their spirits.
> The glimpse of a dazzling male
> Is one cure for impotence.

The Charleston in France

We all know the American music, which brings back so many memories, but many of us have forgotten the words. Very different from the original English words, the French version tells a good deal about Paris in the Twenties, when we analyze it in retrospect.

> She gives the orders now
> She wears the pants now
> And I'm the one who has no say !

Straws in the Wind

" A certain Mme Devilliers, who kept an unpretentious place of business in the Boule-

The Dolly Sisters.

vard Saint-Martin, has just been arrested. She is charged with having provided quarters where elderly gentlemen and very young girls could come together." (From a newspaper.)

In his diary, Maurice Sachs made the following entry in 1929: " I'm tired. I have migraine, my legs feel like lead, and I'm bored. I'm getting old. ' But you aren't thirty yet,' they point out. What they don't seem to realize is that in a period like ours to be thirty is to be terribly old."

Maison Privée

MASSAGES—SOCIAL GATHERINGS
Antinéa at her Occidental
Address
Private House—4, Rue Pigalle

Dada, or The Nothingness Club

Dada, a subject of lively literary discussions between one one-step and the next, was an import from abroad. Its birthplace was Zürich, and no secret was made of the extent to which it was a kind of game.

" When we observe the excesses of the Dadaists, how can we fail to recall the red waistcoats of the Romantics? " wrote Raymond Radiguet shortly after Dada's arrival in Paris. The painter Hans Arp has told of its beginnings in Zürich. " I formally put on record that Tristan Tzara found the word Dada on February 8, 1916 at 6 P.M. My twelve children and I were present when Tzara pronounced the word for the first time, immediately eliciting our well-founded enthusiasm. I am convinced this word is of no importance whatever, and that only idiots

43

and Spanish professors are interested in dates. What we do care about is the Dada spirit, and we were all dada before Dada existed..."

The first publications of the school were printed in Tarenz-bei-Imst, in the Tyrol. The word itself had been discovered by opening a dictionary at random and stabbing the page with a pencil, without looking. Dada thus reflects in its origins something of the atmosphere of that " war of words " which went on in neutral countries during World War I, something of a Switzerland filled with professional spies, adventurers, and political refugees. It was in such a hissing cauldron that the peculiar brew was cooked up, and when Dada reached Paris in 1920 it aroused violent indignation from many, laughter from the uncomprehending, and applause from a few.

Only later was it possible to sum up the movement. "The activity known as Dada represented the permanent revolt of the individual against art, against morality, against society." This is exact. As recently as 1956, a retrospective exhibition devoted to the movement was marked by several episodes of violence. Dada was a kind of battering ram, capable of breaking down more than one kind of wall, of shattering more than one kind of privacy. If many Dada actions resembled the practical jokes of schoolboys, it was not for that any less influential in the world of letters. Cubism, which antedates Dada, had not been in revolt against art, but had claimed to constitute its supreme development. Dada, however, set out to destroy art.

Of all the post-World War I movements in art and letters in which it is possible to observe

◀ *Joséphine Baker, as Henri Laurens saw her.*

...and as the photographer did. ▶

self-destructive tendencies at work—varieties of "revolt" which went beyond mere contempt for the bourgeois as Flaubert had portrayed him, and attacked "beauty," art, syntax, prosody, even the word itself—of all these movements Dada was by far the most important. Cubism and Fauvism, which appeared between 1900 and 1910, had by their success opened the door to every variety of originality, but Dada supplied in addition something they lacked—something which carried it beyond any narrowly literary or artistic relevance—the myth of a revolt against everything.

La Jazzbandette

Two young women are sitting on poufs, chatting, in the thoroughly uncomfortable positions adjudged smart in those days. "What are you planning to do on your wedding night this time?" one of them inquires. "Oh, you know—" the other replies offhandedly, "Something like a good tango."

A good tango?

"At first, he pretended not to notice. Then, seeing that far from being offended, she was in complete accord, he pressed harder against her swaying body, putting his back into it. When he felt her hand leave his shoulder and creep up the back of his neck, the fingers clenching in an unconscious caress, he went wild. Their bodies kept moving, fast against each other; then pitched forward; and to the mechanical ebb and flow of the dance they slowly achieved a repetition of the timeless act..."

Miss (Mistinguett).

At which point the *garçonne*, the "emancipated woman" of Victor Margueritte's novel says to the dancing partner she has just picked up, "You dance very well. Let's try it again."

I'm Looking for Titina

Most often with walls lacquered red, colored spotlights, and revolving mirrored globes to produce the illusion of constantly shifting lights and movement, and with orchestras able to play both jazz numbers and tangos, *les dancings*—places to dance, often too tiny to be called "dance halls" and not as yet exclusively *night* clubs—had been multiplying at a great rate ever since 1919. The principal steps favored were the sinister, complicated Tango, the Fox Trot, the Apache Waltz, and the Charleston. New verbs entered the French language, necessitated by the fact that everyone—men, women, and children—now *fox-trottaient* and *tanguaient* (occasionally, *tangotaient*). People practiced the new steps in the streets, on the way to the office, during dinner. The *garçonne*'s mother was described as "covering many kilometers between her first shimmy at five in the afternoon and her last tango at one in the morning." From the cradle to the grave, at a syncopated sexy brass-blared rhythm.

The dances went like this. The eccentric one-step—one, two, one, two—a compromise between jazz and the military march. It was also called a Rosalie, formerly a front-line nickname for the bayonet. And then the Fox Trot: one step forward and one step back, and to the side—one, two, three times around, and be careful not to make a polka out of it... *Je cherche après Titine...*

And finally the Charleston! Josephine Baker launched it at the Champs-Élysées vaudeville theater. Suddenly, everything became straight lines and angles: the legs went out at sharp angles to the bust, the lower legs raised at the knee to make a right angle with the thighs. The Charleston was the Cubist dance par excellence, its rhythm the very heartbeat of the Style Gomina!

To describe this period atmosphere, writers had to use their muscles. Paul Morand was the most skillful at this, employing a terse, telegraphic style derived from the great poet Blaise Cendrars. Kessel, too, managed to write sentences with the force of a fist to the jaw. At a less exalted—a much less exalted—level, Dekobra had his points; his *Minuit Place Pigalle* is a kind of masterpiece. It is to these writers we must turn if we would recapture these years—also to Raymond Machard and Victor Margueritte. It is in them we make the acquaintance of the " Madonna of the Pullmans," of the woman driven mad by passion, of the aviator and the Legionnaire, of cynical headwaiters in Montmartre night clubs, of the whore who is dressed in rayon from head to foot and is in cahoots with the woman who keeps the toilets—for now the toilet makes its entry into the novel, at the same time the telephone was making its first appearance on the stage—Lewis and Irène, *le sixdayman* (another example of Anglomania), the young man known as " The Baroness "—all these fixtures in the fiction of the Twenties were firmly rooted in observation of ordinary life.

Maurice. ▶

Drawing for a fan by Paul Iribe, from an album published by Paquin.

49

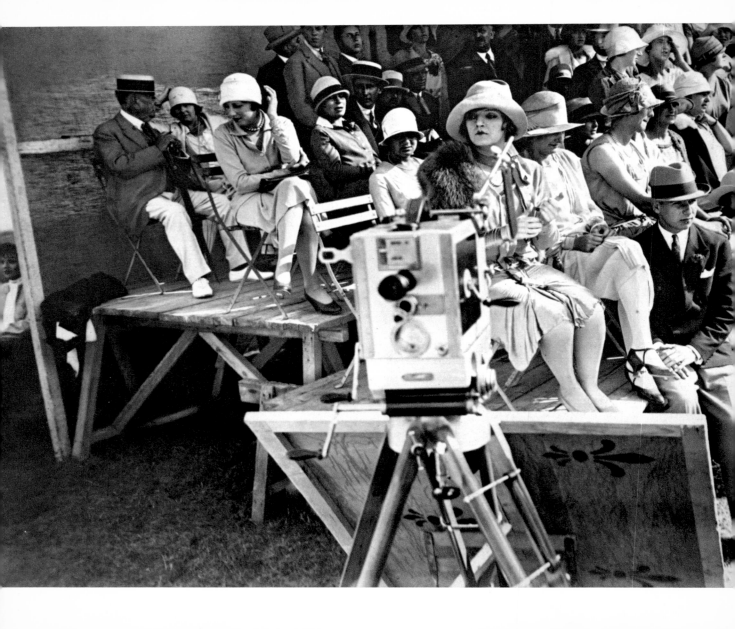

The Twenties literature with its emancipated women left its mark on the masses, for all that the latter were, in general, hostile. The motion pictures, most effectively, urged the common man to imitate modern heroes. Any little bank clerk could now order a bottle of champagne with all the savoir-faire of a Boni de Castellane, or so he began to believe. All he had to do, after all, was to do as they do in the movies. The Twenties in this manner put into real-life circulation a host of stereotyped characters, originating on film: the racetrack gambler, the gangster, the brothel Madam, the bartender, the gigolo, the dealer in cocaine, the short-skirted secretary whisked off in her boss's Rolls-Royce, the cigar-chewing industrialist, the professional prizefighter, the war profiteer, the striped-pants diplomat, the professional dancing partner (this last a phenomenon unique with the Twenties). Ah! Where is the poet to sing the melancholy fate of all those dancing partners suddenly out of a job in 1929?

Keeping Occupied Along the Rhine

Had everyone then forgot all about the War, as they danced away the nights? What a slanderous thought! The Rhineland was under occupation, wasn't it? A bilingual magazine, *La Revue Rhénane*, was at this time somewhat premature in its efforts to bring about closer relations between France and Germany. One number for the year 1923 carried this notice:

"Large assortment of coffins—zinc, white metal, pine, and oak—designed to French specifications (*sic!*). Bodies of soldiers buried

The Movies.

51

in the Rhineland exhumed and shipped. All orders filled promptly, legal formalities included. Supplier to Military Hospital No. 1, Mayence, Postal Sector 77."

Semper Corydon

André Gide was one of the Twenties' most famous men of letters. He was the most Protestant of all French writers—so Protestant, in fact, this frail, balding man whose features were invariably set in a chilly expression, that he falsified the sense of the word. He protested too much; he was gripped by a frenzy of protest. He even protested against the sexual condition of mankind.

The essential part of what he had to say had appeared prior to 1914. For the next quarter of a century he was primarily concerned with the publication of his complete works.

He was an important influence in the *Nouvelle Revue Française* during this period, when it was taking upon itself the role of literary dictator. Leaving to lesser and more ephemeral magazines the publishing of avant-garde, experimental writing, the policy of the N. R. F. was to codify and direct the over-all tendencies of post-war literature. When it began to appear again in 1919, its chiefs of staff included such names as Jacques Rivière, Paul Claudel, Gide, Valéry, Fargue, Duhamel, Proust, etc.

Gide's *André Walter* appeared in 1892, *Les Nourritures Terrestres* in 1897. The date of the *Caves du Vatican* is 1914. The post-war Gide was the Gide of *Corydon*, of *The Counterfeiters*, of the autobiographical *Si le Grain ne meurt* ("If It Die..."). While younger writers were carrying to the furthest extreme their passionate pursuit of originality at all costs, Gide was looking rather for the most fleeting expressions of sincerity. His sincerity, however, is not beyond question. At some point in his career—it would be interesting to know just when—it became exhibitionism, as in these lines from *Corydon*: "One woman does not suffice to make a man happy. Monogamy is out of the question. The only relief for this situation within the framework of our society comes down to pederasty, prostitution, or adultery... Homosexuality is normal. It is *a priori* false that the pederast is effeminate, cowardly, or decadent..."

Son of a jurist, Gide hated the family as an institution. This attitude is comprehensible, for the primary condition of family life is the presence of a wife and mother. He loathed the social framework, was as much anti-social as he was anti-family. His mind soared far above the plane of ordinary human expe-

Charlot.

rience, being really at home only with the universal and the singular, its two extremes.

We may ask whether it was merely a malicious witticism, when someone observed recently that the most lasting achievement of twentieth century literature will have been to make sexual anomalies respectable again? Proust, as is well known, was still reticent enough to call his Albert, the Turkish bath boy, Albertine—thus allowing the ladies among his readers to be taken in, if they so desire. Since Proust, however, the Alberts have come into their own. It used occasionally to be said, at the height of Radiguet's, Cocteau's, and Gide's fame—as Proust lay on his death-bed—that French writers had brought back the days of the court of King René of Anjou (who greatly encouraged letters). It would have been more apt to say the court of Henri III ! Undoubtedly, when 1975 rolls around, and it is time to strike a commemorative medal for the fiftieth anniversary of 1925, the face on the reverse side of the medal will have to be the face of Corydon.

Gide-iana

At one point it became known that Gide was selling a portion of his library, including works which had been inscribed to him by such authors as Francis Jammes, Maurice Maeterlinck, and Henri de Régnier. We might suppose this was a banal enough occasion in the life of a great writer, but in the Twenties reporters and the public followed Gide's

Philippe Hériat in l'Inhumaine, *directed by Marcel l'Herbier. Sets by the future director, Claude Autant-Lara.*

every move in the constant expectation, sometimes rewarded, of being scandalized. *Le Canard Enchaîné* was able to make something even out of this.

" He is only selling off books by writers who turned their backs to him. In the case of Lord Alfred Douglas, who had somewhat earlier turned his back to Oscar Wilde, we understand perfectly, but what about Léon Daudet? And Mme Catulle-Mendès? Or Jean de Bonnefon? Truly, he must have known some very frustrating days ! "

Cinéma-Ciné
(Motion Pictures—Movies)

There were 184 movie houses in Paris in 1925. Pola Negri was appearing in *Mon Homme*, Catherine Hessling in *Nana*—a delectable Nana, all fire and lubricity. Jacques Feyder had just bought the rights to *Thérèse Raquin*. Zola was very much in fashion. Readers of the magazine *Cinéma-Ciné* had voted for their favorite films. The winner (with 1,721 votes) was *Le Miracle des Loups*, a historical romance set in the reign of Louis XI, with acres of papier-mâché sets. Chaplin's *Le Pèlerin* (" The Pilgrim ") was second with 1,650 votes, and *La Terre Promise* (" The Covered Wagon ") third with 1,363 votes. For all its adjustment to entertainment in rather small, dark halls, the public had kept its taste for epic grandeur, and despite the low quality of most movie narratives, its respect for excellence.

It is noteworthy that two of the films were American, indicating the inroad of a cosmopolitanism which already had gone quite far. And could go absurdly far, as in this naive publicity release for a Russian film about the great English actor *Kean*: " A film very much in the French tradition, directed by Wolkoff and played by Mosjoukine, Koline, and Lissenko."

René Clair's *Entr'acte* was shown at the *Arts Décos* exposition. A little masterpiece of the ludicrous, it was very well received. But the two film personalities who were filling the movie houses were Zigoto (Larry Semon) and Harold Lloyd (known in France as *Lui*).

Harold Lloyd has them lined up at the box office. Harold Lloyd is inimitable. Harold Lloyd is the Prince of Clowns. Everyone adores Harold Lloyd. A gold mine to his producers.

Obviously, the publicity departments of the studios were already unbiased in praise of their stars! However, Abel Gance, the French director who had just released *La Roue* (" The Wheel ") and was starting work on *Napoléon*, was nonetheless optimistic about the future of the cinema. " It will endow us with an extra sense: we will learn to listen with our eyes. The cinema will develop something like what prosody is to poetry—a versification in light. We will follow the conversation of the birds, and what the wind says. A railroad track will acquire the force of music. A single wheel will appear as lovely as a Greek temple. The age of the image is here."

Well—to a certain extent, it was.

For all its justifiable claims to the status of an art, however, the motion picture could not really do without its appeal as spectacle, as mass entertainment. The movie house pianist of the silent era, banging away on his broken-down upright to accompany the flickerings of light on the screen above him, remains a preposterous, albeit a charming figure. And in the day of the talkies, the sub-titles are frequently as hilariously funny as the French dialogue placed in the mouths of American cowboy characters (by the process known in French as doubling). " Not for all the gold in the world," says the ingénue, " would I touch one penny of your money."

But movies in the Twenties meant, above all others, Rudolf Valentino. This little Italian immigrant to the United States, who had become a Hollywood star, exercised an incredible fascination. Details of his private life were published over and over again.

Saint Valentino

In January, 1926, Valentino was in Paris to attend the charity première of his film *The Black Eagle*. He had come over a month earlier, and, as Jany Casanova told it, a little girl who was gravely ill had been miraculously cured simply by catching sight of him. Rudy went to see the little girl and told her, " I am happy to have had the power to cure you, and I am more flattered by it than by all the compliments I have ever received."

Charlot

The post-war years recognized that Chaplin possessed genius. It was impossible to deny his clairvoyance. The famous cane, the baggy trousers, the battered derby set carefully over the tight mop of curls, and the ritual fade-out of the little tramp walking away, the soles of

Antinéa (see p. 22). *Poiret's assimilation of the joint influences of Pierre Benoit and Diaghilev. Drawing by Lepape.*

his ridiculous shoes flapping in the dust—all this evoked loud admiration, and deservedly so.

Jean Cocteau tried to explain it: " Charlie Chaplin, alias Charles Chaplin, alias Charlot, alias Karl, alias Chap, depending on the country and background of his admirers, deserves a long study all to himself, and I mean to write it. This comedian, this tragedian even, this acrobat, is playing somewhere all the time. Reports of his death are frequently given out. Maybe he is dead. Is he English, American, Spanish, French, or Russian? People fight over where he was born. As Georges Courteline would have said, he is a fellow in the Homer category."

Cendrars was also quick to grasp the legendary dimensions of the pantomimist. " I saw Charlot. It was he, all right. He was a poor student I shared a room with in London around 1911, a poor little medical student who read Schopenhauer all day long and at night went on in a music hall to collect his nightly ration of kicks in the rear, the same music hall where Simon Kra, today a publisher, triumphed as world's champion at diabolo, and where I had a juggling act myself, with both hands—for I still had two hands then."

What the Twenties did not yet grasp was that underlying Charlot's slapstick were some fairly harsh indictments of modern society. Over and beyond the custard pie aspect of his comedy, inherited from the Mack Sennett days, was another which came to flower in *The Immigrant*, in the comedies where he played soldier, and in the unforgettable ballet of the rolls in *The Gold Rush;* whenever the clown portrayed real hunger, was caught up

Tristan Tzara kissing the hand of Nancy Cunard at one of the Count de Beaumont's charity balls.

in the eternal mirage of the child-woman, or looked closely at peculiar features of modern life. Before long, he was to portray with frightening symbolic force a multimillionaire who could only recognize his old buddy when he was drunk !

Without saying a word, the Charlot of the silent films bore eloquent witness against the savagery of the Twentieth Century.

Genius for Suicide

To make a demigod of the great clown Chaplin was one means whereby the post-war epoch managed not to think about its suicides, which included such notable figures as Max Linder, Jacques Vaché, and—somewhat later—René Crevel. I have been leafing through a file of the magazine *La Révolution Surréaliste*, and have open before me the page on which photographs of twenty-eight young men have been set around one of the anarchist Germaine Berton, as an expression of solidarity with her.

I cannot look for very long at the face of René Crevel, at those features suggesting a prizefighter of unusual sensibility, without being deeply moved, as by the photograph of an elder brother who has died. There is a flick of the whip in his expression, in the broad jaw and the heavy eyebrows that overshadow the eyes. The expression was only a mask, however, behind which lurked the solitariness of a Chaplin, the despair of a Vaché, and Max Linder's mortal boredom.

The photograph was taken in December, 1924, in conjunction with one of those questionnaires his Surrealist friends were so fond of, this particular one being headed, " Is Suicide a Solution? " Crevel's reply was,

"The era of temporary fun and games is just about over." And the Surrealists concluded, "If suicide were a solution, we would be proud and happy to drive the world to commit it."

Had Crevel any suspicion that ten years later he would himself furnish a few lines of newsprint, like the reports of suicides printed in *La Révolution Surréaliste?* The memory of René Crevel is precious to me, as is that of Robert Desnos: they never compromised. They had nothing of the Gide about them—whose elaborately sophistic anecdote on suicide was quoted by Jean Paulhan in the same number. "One day a man was found with his throat cut, lying in his own bed. On a little table next to it was a piece of paper with these words written on it: " I had a dream that I was doing away with myself, and when I awoke I discovered that it was true."

Once again, Gide was cheating: suicide does not lend itself to humor, however true the reverse of that statement may be. Crevel believed in the Surrealist revolution; it never came off. Ten years later, he chose to die.

Jacques Vaché, Modigliani, Max Linder, Pascin—men such as these were the dark angels of the Twenties.

The Exquisite Corpse

Paris in the Twenties cannot be comprehended without the Surrealist ferment in

◄ *Undersea Ball. Collage by the Count de Beaumont.*

Ornamental Ironwork? No—Jewels by Cartier. ►

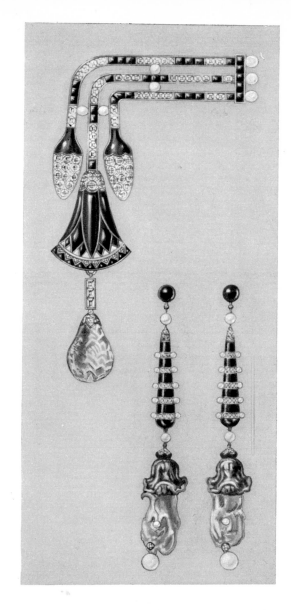

literature and the arts. Developed out of Dada, it was for a time difficult to distinguish where the one stopped and the other began. Aragon, for example, at one point spoke of a " vice called Surrealism, a passionately disorganized use of the astonishing image."

André Breton supplied the official definition. " Surrealism: (masc. noun), Pure psychic automatism by means of which it is proposed to express in either spoken or written language, or by any other means whatever, the real functioning of thought. Thought dictated to the mind in the absence of control exercised by reason, without reference to any aesthetic or moral consideration."

A continuation of Dada, influenced by Freudianism and revolutionary in spirit, Surrealism made researches into the elemental expression of the preconscious mind. The earliest Surrealist writings consisted almost entirely of accounts of dreams. Automatic writing, the best-known of the Surrealist techniques, was for them a means of " opening out to infinity the succession of Chinese boxes within boxes that is called mankind."

They made strenuous efforts to write without conscious reflection, to record the succession of images that appear to the mind.

André Breton, Paul Eluard, Philippe Soupault, and Benjamin Péret underwent experiments in simulation of all the major psychotic states as generally diagnosed: acute mania, general paralysis, dementia praecox, etc. Even before the Surrealists took up the " ready-made " object, they had invented the " object-being." The latter consisted of some misshapen thing found anywhere, upon which another unlikely object might be grafted. Picasso and Dali were especially skillful at this. Meanwhile, a Surrealist parlor game was invented, " The Exquisite Corpse." " The game consists of a folded piece of paper upon which a sentence or a drawing is composed by several persons, none of whom is aware of what has been written or drawn by those who have already contributed. The classic example, which gave the game its name, was the very first sentence obtained in this way: *Le cadavre—exquis—boira—le vin—nouveau.*"

The Gertrude Hoffman Girls on an Outing at Auteuil.

Clocking Despair

Around 1910, Cubism suddenly struck the bourgeois amateur of painting and literature as " more original " than Futurism, its immediate predecessor. In 1917, the half-serious, half-clowning exercise in undermining that was Dada seemed to be a " progression " beyond Cubism. For more than a century the history of art and letters had been sub-

Ladies' Heels.

jected to this sort of auction-room bidding. At the tail end of Romanticism, Lautréamont; after him, Baudelaire; and then Rimbaud; after Rimbaud, Jarry; and then Marinetti, Apollinaire, Cubism, Dada, and Surrealism at intervals of a few years only. These successive waves of assault affected the very structure of language—and the language of music and painting as well as that of poetry.

Syntax was badly hit; the sentence was consumed. The end result was automatic writing and the simulation of pathological

states. Although Freudian discoveries legitimized all such experiments, their widespread elaboration in the Twenties was dizzying. James Joyce and a few others were even breaking up the word. Languages, and not only the French language, were tending to pure onomatopoeia; painting was moving toward the spot of color; music was rejoining untempered sound. We know today where they were heading: toward Lettrisme, Abstract Painting and Tachisme, Concrete Music. But what was easy for music, and at least possible in painting, was impossible in letters.

This road could lead only to disaster. How can one possibly go beyond the Madman—unless by ending up as the Mute or the Corpse?

Nonetheless, the Surrealists did find a way out. By adding a suffix to " revolt," the key term that Dada had spawned, they temporarily and partially escaped utter impasse. Logically enough, the Surrealists decided to affiliate with Communism. It was the one way out that led back into the public world. " These young bourgeois," as Aragon called himself and his friends, struggled for four years on the fringes of revolutionary politics, not without arousing the contempt of the professionals.

Recourse to " the revolution " saved the Surrealists from suicide or apostasy, but it had its own tragic consequences. These young men raised on Lautréamont, Rimbaud, and Jarry, were disorganized by vocation. Their literary renunciation of all discipline had simply confirmed them more strongly in their individualism. The brick wall they beat their heads against was their hope—

Commodore Poiret at work.

doomed, for another generation at least, to be unsuccessful—of fusing Freudianism with Marxism. Gradually the movement was torn to shreds within itself as the Twenties gave

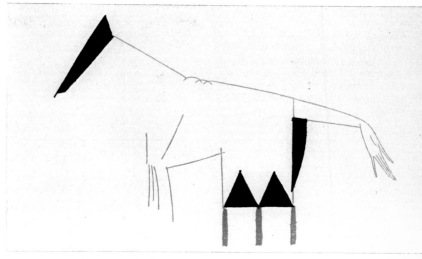

Drawing by Lepape.

way to the Thirties and the whole world began once more to writhe in agony.

The Capital of Insult

In the area of personal invective, the Surrealists' fundamental tenet of " Scandal for scandal's sake " led them to unqualified success. Paris in the Twenties was the world capital of insult.

" Dogs trained to mulct the nation to the maximum, just thinking about a bone like this to gnaw on has you wagging your tails already." *(Révolution d'abord et toujours.)*

65

And here are a few excerpts from Breton's reply to Joseph Delteil, after the latter had written him asking him to arrange an interview with a reporter. "Thank you for the Rumanian newspaperman, but I already have my hands full with aggressive bores *(enmerdeurs)* of every variety. Among whom, these past few months, I must say I am obliged to number you, Joseph Delteil. Confidentially, your *Jeanne d'Arc* was a crock of shit... The only question that remains in my mind about you is whether you are a dirty swine or a moldy cunt—or a dirty swine and a moldy cunt...—André Breton."

It is impossible to pass over in silence this extraordinary proliferation in the Twenties of the insult treated as a Fine Art.

The Wonders of the Arts Décos

Like every other World's Fair, the *Arts Décos* international exposition opened while workmen were still crawling around on scaffolding and nothing seemed ready. The official opening was July 18, 1925. People were prompt to make a pun: *L'Exposition des Arts Décors hâtifs* (hasty), instead of *Arts Décoratifs.* The public of the Twenties clung to the Nineties habit of making little plays on words where public personalities and events were concerned.

Gaston Doumergue, president of the Repub-

◀ *Pre-War Survival. Gouache by Paul Iribe.*

Lacquer panels by Dunand. ▶

lic, led the official party on opening day. Chubby but spry, " Gastounet " in his cocked hat was saluted by porters in gold braid as he headed for the Pavilion of Elegance over the very same Cours-la-Reine where the Farmers-General in the eighteenth century had entertained Manon with a ballet, with dancers from the Opéra. The symbolic significance of things always escaped Gastounet. Four dressmakers carried off the honors—Callot, Jenny, Lanvin, and Worth—amid the alarm-

As Time Goes By.

ing animal life of Siegel's attenuated mannequins. It was like some exotic Riviera garden set with cactus, a plant that according

to Alexandre Jakowsky was the botanical totem of Cubism. The Soviet Pavilion stood opposite that of *L'Intransigeant;* in 1937 it would stand opposite that of Germany. Nobody was as yet worried about Communism, save for a few " conservatives, " men like Bailby and Fabry. The Tower of Paris rose above the Esplanade des Invalides, its loudspeaker blaring.

Gastounet must have been a trifle befuddled before long, what with the Negro music, the dazzling jewels in the diamond merchants' display, Mallet Steven's reinforced concrete trees and the big department stores with workshops on exhibit: the goddesses Pomona for upholstery and Primavera for the arts and crafts of the Negro, and the Masterly Skill of the Galeries Lafayette (Style Gomina), presenting an ideal apartment for Lewis and Irène, Paul Morand's "young marrieds" of the epoch.

Picasso's Metamorphoses

Low of brow, eyebrows knitted in the perpetual scowl of the Malagan peasant, with one dark love-lock forever falling over his temple, Picasso is as crafty as he is brilliant. Where twentieth-century myths are concerned, his influence has been as great as Apollinaire's.

From youth on, his energies have been too multifarious to hold his talent within the usual confines of a painter's career. He was always attracted by the trickery aspect of art, its illusionism, and by the techniques of copying and imitation. Struggling against his weakness—a weakness shared by many painters—he carried his respect for material

Two Women. *Painting by Fernand Léger.*

appearances so far as to incorporate fragments of this kind of " reality " in his paintings: real sand, bits of wood and cork, sandpaper, newsprint, bottle labels. He was the first painter to do this systematically.

Like a bullfighter, he has always appreciated the value of a sudden reversal of direction: Picasso's only uniformity as an artist lies in the constant changes that have marked the development of his art. By the time his mastery of the Toulouse-Lautrec period style was being recognized, he had already moved on to the acrobats and strolling players of his " rose " and " blue " styles. Borrowing Harlequin from the Commedia dell'Arte, adding a window, a guitar, and an empty pack of cigarettes—presto !—Picasso has invented Cubism. It happened in 1907, at Céret. But he did not remain a Cubist long; soon he was in his Negro period, then his Pre-Colombian and Aztec periods, and so on... With certain portraits he has created a new-model Venus—crumbling, dissolving, going up in flames—and he also created so indubitably great a work as *Guernica*, surely the peak of his long career. It is said that he has always been a great frequenter of galleries, forever keen to see what the youngest and newest painters are doing, anxious lest he be outdistanced. Abstract painting, it is said, bothers him a good deal; its mounting success is supposed to be felt by him as a threat to his legendary, all but primordial fame.

Picasso told the following story to André Warnod one day. "Do you remember that head of a bull I had in my last show? I'll tell you how it was conceived. One day I noticed in a corner the handle-bar and the seat of a bicycle, lying in such a way as to look like

Post Card.

Hispano-Suiza.

a bull's head. I picked them up and put them together so that nobody could possibly fail to realize that this seat and this handle-bar from a bike were really a bull's head. My metamorphosis was successful, and now I wish there could be another one, this time in reverse. Suppose that one day my head of a bull were to be thrown on a junk heap. Maybe a little boy would come along and notice it and say to himself, 'Now there's something I could use as a handle-bar for my bike.' If that ever happens, we will have brought off a double metamorphosis."

This modern supplement to Ovid is Picasso's life in a nutshell.

Montparno's Blues

In the Twenties, painting was even more vigorously pursued and widely commented upon than music or poetry. Upon demobilization, both French and foreign artists gravitated to Paris in numbers greater than ever before. Cubism, Fauvism, Dada, and the Surrealism of the Twenties were known,

71

but not yet famous or widely recognized as major revolutions in art. That this situation changed rapidly can be understood better by recalling the economic background. Inflation and easy money made an artist's life relatively cheap and comfortable in France. At this time wine was plentiful and conversation stimulating. From the end of World War I down to the terrible Wall Street crash of 1929—between the death of Modigliani, the black swan of Livorno, the Tristan of Montparnasse, and the suicide of Pascin in Montmartre—conditions were unusually favorable for art.

It was at this time that the cafés formerly called "bistros" were transformed into "bars." Chambon, a native of Auvergne and the owner of the *Dôme*, had to enlarge his establishment. Among the fixtures of the place was a real Redskin, whose name was Gitche Manitou. No single establishment sums up Montparnasse in its heyday better than the *Dôme*. A contemporary described it as "at one and the same time, our community center, our public square, our inn, our forum, our auction room, our ghetto, and our Court of Miracles." The prettiest young models were always to be found there, stockingless, with different kinds of flowers painted on their legs: roses, daisies, bachelor buttons, pinks. The number of "joints" increased enormously. The *Jockey* was superseded by the *Jungle*—a significant change of name. Shortly, a group of artists would be calling themselves "The Horde." Never, since the days of the "Mohicans of Paris," had there been such a vogue for the wild, for the "savage"—so long, of course, as it was properly housebroken.

House Party in the Country. *Painting by Van Dongen.*

Where, only a few years before, a starving Soutine had wandered the streets, stopping to rest against the walls of buildings, dreaming of the insides of butcher shops, and where a drunken Modigliani had screamed out his lungs, now women in mink coats (then as now the favorite fur) had themselves driven up to the entrances of places like the *Dôme* in Hispano-Suizas as long as locomotives. As the uniformed chauffeur would get out and come around to open the door, all heads on the terrace would turn for a good look at the legs of the elegant creature getting out.

On a December night in 1927, one Fraux, originally from Quercy, opened *La Coupole*, a new café-bar built where until recently had stood the establishment of a dealer in coal and lumber named Juglar. Fraux was a friend of Anatole de Monzie and Pierre Benoit. It was announced that there would be a dance floor in the basement. Montparnasse had come a long way from the sleepy, red-wine drinking village of yesterday—a long way since it ordered its first gin fizz, its first Scotch, its first cocktail. There was fierce competition between *Le Dôme* and *La Coupole* as soon as the latter opened. To a lavish use of nickel was soon added red (imitation) leather seats, and finally neon lighting.

Until 1924, when Michel-Georges Michel, a newspaperman, published his novel about the tragic life and death of Modigliani, nobody had ever thought of calling the citizens of Montparnasse *les Montparnos*. The novel became a popular success and after that its author was no longer welcome at the café terraces of Montparnasse—but what did he care? He was a professional, and besides he had changed a word; to a writer it is little things like that that count.

But simpler-minded readers in the provinces were less disdainful, and they came in droves for a glimpse of Picasso, Van Dongen, or Foujita at the *Rotonde*—much as their children would flock to the sacred triangle formed by the *Lipp*, the *Deux Magots*, and the *Flore* at Saint-Germain-des-Prés for a glimpse of Sartre or Camus in 1947. It is interesting that in the Twenties Montparnasse had its sacred triangle too—the *Rotonde*, the *Dôme*, and the *Coupole*—thus verifying Euclid's law about the equivalence of certain three-sided forms.

Chambon took over active management of the *Dôme* and was highly successful in keeping it filled with painters and their models. Never before had Montparnasse known such prosperity. You would see Kiki there often, regally beautiful, incredibly foul-mouthed. Youki Foujita, a lovely Flemish blonde, gave Kiki stiff competition, however. Voronov monkey-gland experiments were much discussed. "New Horizons Have Opened Up," was *L'Illustration*'s innocent heading. But there was a good deal of talk about politics, too: about Poincaré, Briand, disarmament, wheat futures, stocks on the Bourse. And Einstein's theory of relativity. People would remember that only a few years before, Lenin and Trotsky had frequented this very café, and waiters would be asked to point out where they used to sit. "They don't always point out the same seats," observed Pierre Humbourg.

Fraux hired a Hindu in native costume to give the *Dôme*'s American Indian some competition. Among other foreign visitors attracted by the bright lights of Montparnasse were James Joyce, whose *Ulysses* had been published in Paris in 1922, Hemingway (before he

The Champions.

Deauville.

let his beard grow), and Henry Miller, who made his first appearance in 1928, with his buddies Alfred Perlès, Florent Fels, and Cendrars. More and more Anglo-Americans kept pouring in, challenging the earlier numerical superiority of the Germans and the Russians. If Montparnasse had made many think of Central Europe, by the time it was called " Montparno " it had changed its orientation. Now it faced the Atlantic.

The Lady Poet and The Painter

Anna de Noailles (as Foujita puts the finishing touches to his portrait of her): " But you haven't made my eyes big enough. My eyes have been compared to broad flowing rivers. And what have you done to my forehead? Make it broader and higher. I'm a poet—what

Women Bathing. *Painting by Raoul Dufy.*

do you suppose I do my thinking with? This portrait has got to be just right—it will be all anyone knows of how I look, after I'm dead. After all, my friend, one of these days I *will* be dead."

Foujita (between clenched teeth): " Yes."

Love and Gasoline

The automobiles of the Twenties no longer resembled the " putt-putts " of 1900, as Morand described them. He himself ordered a custom sports chassis for a 20 h.p. motor from Panhard, a firm reported as " letting him have it for 59,000 francs." Rather, the automobile now took on the attributes of heroes and heroines in novels. In Pierre Frondaie's *L'Homme à l'Hispano*, the auto *was* a character in its own right—and perhaps more truly alive and real than the people in that book. However, the streets were not as yet jammed bumper to bumper. An accident resulting in only one death could still be given a full column on the first page of *L'Intran*. A gang of crooks with a car at their disposition struck the public imagination as the biggest thing since " the Bonnot gang." Policemen on bicycles had surprised the gang, and they had fled in their car ! " Innumerable businessmen now have their own little cars. It said in the papers the other day that a schoolteacher's car overturned on a road in the Haute-Loire. ' The schoolteacher's car.' Up to now we had only heard people in country districts speak of ' the priest's car ' and ' the doctor's car.' This is indeed Progress."

The 1925 models of the Renault were bright yellow or blood red, with hood and radiator

Bathing Beauties.

shaped like the muzzle of some great beast. Two chauffeurs up front, and in the back—far, far to the back—the passengers. Gérard Bauer waxed witty on this theme. " At the stern of this energetic and adaptable coupé rises a transparent turret with room for two. Room for no more than two. Love could have no more splendid chariot than this."

Advertising took a new turn. Two cars were shown as two pretty young women, heads shaped like the fronts of cars. They are talking. " What we really need, my dear, is a man we can count on, one who will never ditch us. Someone responsive and energetic, yet sensitive and available."

And then there was the Solex brand of carburetor, rigged out in evening clothes, with a monocle. " You lovely creatures, here I am."

But capping them all, the Eiffel Tower now blazed with fire every night: an enormous red flame at the top with heraldic designs in electric light up and down the pylons on two sides. The dates 1889-1925 were spelled out, while huge white stars with golden tails shot dizzily back and forth, their comet-like backwash forming letters running vertically down the Tower. Visitors from the provinces stood gaping at the spectacle, finally making out the magical name of one of the truly great of the epoch:

CITROËN

P. S. to the Future

Eugène Brieux, the playwright who wrote *Les Avariés* (Damaged Goods), set up an annual prize for the best play to treat social problems in a serious and constructive manner.

The prize was not awarded in 1925, because there were no plays of that type given that year.

See France First!

" Frenchmen, spend your holidays in France. Elsewhere you will find an unfavorable exchange, and excessive customs duties. Why go to Switzerland, for example, where your franc is only worth 25 centimes? "

Economics of Prosperity

At the close of the first World War, France had been bled dry—not only by enormous losses on the battlefield, but also economically. However, France did not want to face this fact. She preferred to pretend not to care, to want to forget the horrors of a war which had cost her as dearly as it cost conquered Germany.

The enormous expansion of the artistic avant-gardes who had worked in relative obscurity down to 1918 was closely paralleled by a revolution in economic life, and both of these were paralleled by the revolution in manners. It is possible to view the Twenties vogue for advanced painting, the steady fall of the franc throughout the same period, and the new freedom in social habits, as three aspects of a single phenomenon.

The value of money had declined throughout the war years, more or less in proportion to the quantities of blood being shed—although this latter type of national wealth is not, of course, listed on the Bourse. People with money became increasingly afraid that their wealth was illusory, a situation that led to inflation, and produced a phony prosperity. Money was made more rapidly than ever before, but then it had also to be spent or invested more quickly. Prior to 1914, France had been economically healthy, slow to spend capital, and confident that a franc would still be worth a franc in five years' time—perhaps even a few centimes more. When investments turned out badly—as in the case of investments in Russian enterprises—the French investor paid up and took his loss. The whole country did not panic. The currency was sound. From 1919 on, however, this conviction of essential stability disappeared—at least, within the inner circles of finance, among those " in the know," the real operators. Contemporaries were literally appalled as they came to realize this, for since the days of Louis Philippe the contrary attitude had prevailed, and not even the disaster of 1870 had seriously shaken it.

But the unhealthy economy of the Twenties, inflationary in character, explains the boom in the arts. There is an economic explanation for such phenomena as Montparnasse's unprecedented prosperity, for the way the highest circles of Paris society and the arts flocked to *Le Bœuf sur le Toit*, for the continuing survival of so lavish an enterprise as the Ballets Russes, for the willingness of publishers to take chances on unknown or experimental writers, for the boom in modern painting. It is simply this, that since nobody could be sure what his money would be worth tomorrow, the wisest thing seemed to be to spend it immediately on something offering a quick return. Doubtless to finance a night club, to buy a publishing house, or to collect and store quantities of new paintings, represents a

Head of Man Smoking. *Painting by Joan Miró.*

80

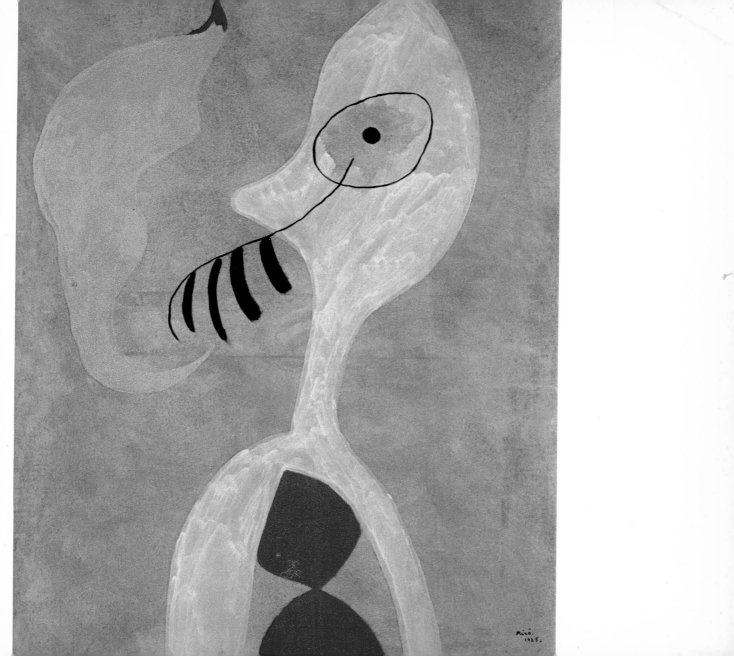

risky type of investment. However, it was the kind of investment that appealed to what used to be called " new " wealth—i.e., wealth consisting solely of money. (The *mercanti*, or war-enriched businessmen of the Twenties, corresponded to the *b. o. f.* of post-World War II. The letters stand for the French words for butter-eggs-cheese.) A canvas by Modigliani, valued at 600 francs before his death, was worth 6,000 francs a few months after his death, and had gone up to 300,000 francs a year or two later. This deadly sort of mathematics underlies all the characteristic phenomena of the Twenties.

It is no wonder that the number of painters multiplied, and that they produced enormous quantities of work. Hitherto, there had been no real market for drawings and sketches, but now even they became a significant part of the art-dealers' activity, pressed by a clientèle with money to spend. Meanwhile the painters themselves, a generally cheerful lot who like to gather together in cafés once the light has gone, spent money in the cafés, turning their three principal Montparnasse hangouts—the *Dôme*, the *Rotonde*, and the *Coupole*—into permanent exhibitions of their work.

Max in Black and White

Bottle imp with monocle, Max Jacob beat a regular path from Montmartre to Montparnasse and back again. Through the veins of this son of generations of Jewish tailors, who was born in Brittany to a mother originally from Avignon, ran the life blood of the Twenties. At once simple-minded and cunning, straightforward and an outrageous liar,

Relâche. *Ballet by Picabia and Satie.*

and singularly ill-adapted to Parisian ways, Max became one of the wizards of the age. After his conversion to Catholicism—a conversion, it is rumored, that nearly cost his confes-

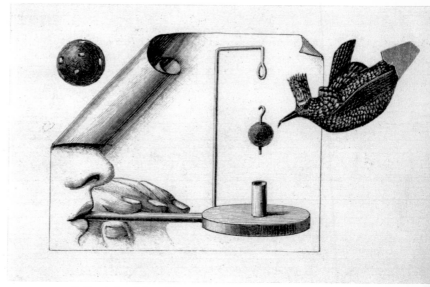

Collage by Max Ernst.

sor his life—he took up the life of a lay brother in the monastery of Saint-Benoît-sur-Loire, where he tried to make up in piety for his earlier abandonment to worldly wickedness. Max's life is best rendered in chiaroscuro, being a matter of extremes which met frequently in him. He could be as unrestrained a sinner as he was genuinely exalted by religion; his Montmartre style of clowning (which ought perhaps to be localized still more closely, as a Rue Ravignan style of clowning) was as infectiously high-spirited as his death

in a German concentration camp was wretched. He and Paul Claudel were the only two French poets of the age to have laid eyes upon the Virgin. The fact that it was in the subway that Max saw her is beside the point.

The Wicked South Side

From his eyrie atop the Butte Montmartre, Max Jacob kept track of all that was going on down in Montparnasse, all the way across Paris. He knew its days were numbered.

"To the South lies a sink of iniquity. Montparnasse lies in its sin. There is evil in the studios of Montparnasse. I have spent the day there, in my black suit, my pumps, and my lace socks. In the evening, when I was taking the subway back, a voice spoke to me quite loudly: 'You who come to me, why do you drive me away from you?'"

After experiences of this kind, the poet who called himself "Brother Matorel" scrawled on the wall of his apartment in the Rue Ravignan: "*Never go to Montparnasse.*"

Another Surrealist Scandal

In 1925 the writers and artists banded together as Surrealists published a protest against the war in Morocco, where the French Army was attempting to exterminate rebels against French rule. The poet Paul Claudel took it upon himself to disassociate himself from French poets capable of so unpatriotic an

Seated: Paul Eluard, Jacques Rigaut, Mic Soupault, Ribemont-Dessaignes.
Standing : Marc Chadourne, Tristan Tzara, Philippe Soupault, Charchoune.

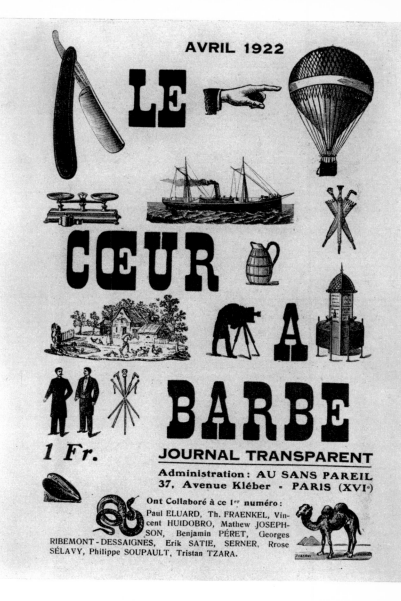

attitude. When they heard this, the Surrealists wrote " An Open Letter to Paul Claudel," which they had printed on shiny red "butcher" paper. It included this sentence: " We formally declare that treason and everything else that might harm this country's security are more easily reconcilable with poetry than the sale of ' great quantities of bacon ' to the account of a nation of mad dogs and swine." (Claudel had made the tactical error of boasting of his own activities as a purchasing agent abroad during World War I.)

During this same year, the Surrealists planned a dinner in honor of the birthday of Saint-Pol-Roux, an elderly gentleman of the Symbolist generation, whose poetry they admired. They chose for the occasion the upstairs dining room of the *Closerie des Lilas*, a quiet, dignified, old fashonied café-restaurant on the fringes of Montparnasse. Mme Rachilde, a contemporary of Saint-Pol-Roux and herself a novelist and editor of the pre-World War I days, was to preside over the festivities. One may gain some idea of this lady's personality from her reply to a question asked in the pages of *Les Nouvelles Littéraires*. The question was, with what heroes of fiction would she identify herself closely enough to want to live their lives as described. Mme Rachilde answered, " With the heroes of my own novels. They all live passionately." Among her novels are such titles as *Le Grand Seigneur* (Lord of the Manor), *Le Meneur de Louves* (Drover of She-Wolves), *L'Heure Sexuelle* (Eros Tells Time), *Le Hors-Nature* (Outlawed by Nature), *Monsieur Vénus*, and *Refaire l'Amour* (Remake Love).

86

Harlequin, 1924. *Watercolor by Fernand Léger.*

Pavlova and Nijinsky. Diaghilev in right background.

Florent Fels sat next to André Breton, and the atmosphere was charged with the recent exchange of pleasantries with Paul Claudel. Mme Rachilde was addressing the gathering.

" That respectable lady is really making a bloody fool of herself," observed Florent Fels, speaking quite clearly, in a voice normally loud.

" For many years now, Monsieur," continued André Breton, " that lady has been a bloody fool."

Saint-Pol-Roux, the guest of honor, inter-

vened chivalrously. As soon as the first seditious remarks had been made, he climbed up onto his chair and shouted, " I am a native of Camaret, a region of seafaring men; I am captain of this ship, and I order you to be seated ! "

At this point, Robert Desnos jumped up and swung by his hands from a curtain rod, with his feet managing to knock over the dining table. As the guests became more and more excited, a crowd began to gather outside the *Closerie*, wondering at the noise.

87

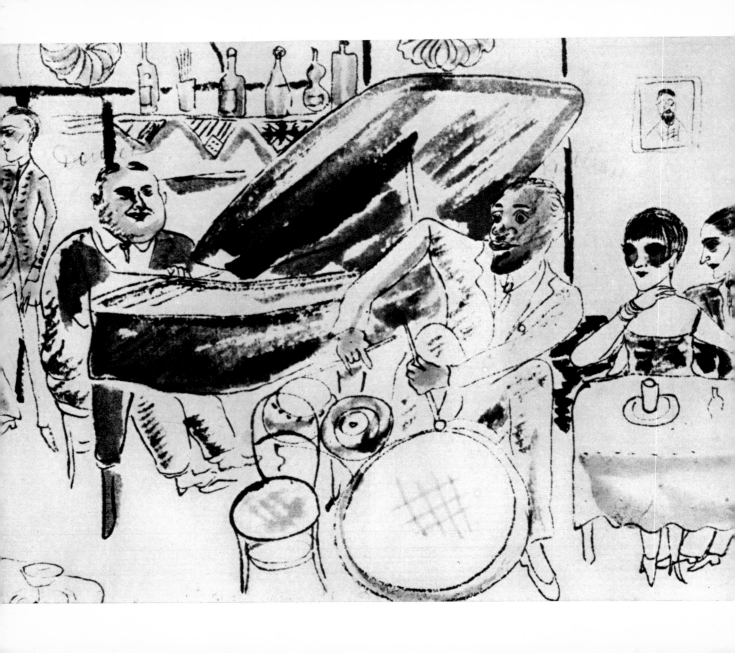

Max Ernst, one of the leading Surrealist painters and still at this time a German national, yelled down to the crowd outside: " Down with Germany ! "

Naturally, the crowd loved this, and cheered. Then a French Surrealist, Michel Leiris, went to the window and yelled " Down with France ! " He and Max Ernst were, of course, saying the same thing. It was a Surrealist principle to place oneself above so vulgar a sentiment as patriotism.

By this time Saint-Pol-Roux, the guest of honor, had collapsed, and Mme Rachilde had screamed herself hoarse. Also, a large mirror had been broken, and the management of the *Closerie*, whose ideas of a literary dinner had been formed on the model of those given by Paul Fort, the Prince of Poets, called the police.

Among others hauled to the police station was Michel Leiris, whom the police had some trouble rescuing from the crowd. Desnos hurriedly got in touch with Edouard Herriot, one of the leading politicians of the day and one who, like Anatole de Monzie, could be relied on to understand post-war literary movements. These were the days of scandal for scandal's sake—a tradition which has almost entirely disappeared in this atomic age when obeying the rules of social convention is the key to success. Perhaps the last such occasion occurred a few years ago, when Michel Mourre yelled out " God is dead ! " in front of the great altar of Notre-Dame. This combination of earnestness, desire to shock, and exhibitionism seems peculiar to us today, but it was altogether normal in the Paris of the Twenties.

Le Bœuf sur le Toit. Jacques Doucet at the piano. Drawing from Foujita's diary.

Artists

" We no longer have any need to call ourselves ' artists,' and may as well leave the term to those who find it glamorous—the hairdressers and the chiropodists."
—Erik Satie

Van Dongen

Standing in front of Van Dongen's dreadful portrait of Anatole France, an old woman commented, " Yes, that's how he used to look, all right. I've often seen him like that, standing in the street watching the little girls coming out of school ! "

As Kiki has noted, it was only so long as his models and their clothes seemed out of style that Kees Van Dongen's art was itself out of fashion. However, we feel more tenderly toward the Twenties today, and its styles of dress and figure have (so to speak) cleared customs at last. We realize now that Van Dongen was not at all a flatterer of his age, but rather one of its sternest moralists; not a party to its absurdities, but a ferocious critic of them; a Daumier of the smart set, more savage than Gavarni. Using color like the flick of a whip, merely by his treatment of the eyes, he could make the woman of the Twenties give herself away. The true moralist of the epoch was not Clément Vautel—what a splendid subject to assign for Beaux-Arts competitions: *Stupidiy Driving Out Vice*—but Van Dongen, portraitist extraordinary to the ladies-who-didn't-want-babies.

One day on the terrace of the *Dôme*, a pretty model came up to him and asked, " Monsieur Van Dongen, tell me why, in one

89

The School of Paris (music). Left to right: Germaine Tailleferre, Francis Poulenc, Arthur Honegger, Darius Milhaud, Jean Cocteau, and Georges Auric.

of your pictures, you painted a dog green? There aren't any green dogs."

He replied, " You are perfectly right, Madame. But will you tell me something, now? Why is your hair tinted lavender? "

The following is reportedly his own. " When I left Holland and came to Paris, I didn't have a sou. I founded an academy of painting so as to have pupils who would pay me. This academy was very helpful to my future, for some of my pupils had a lot of talent." The source for this is Jean Oberlé, who got his start on the old *Crapouillot*. And, now that the name of that magazine has come up, this is as good a place as any to

Drawing (Le mauvais lieu) *by Jean Cocteau, with the artist in the foreground.*

PREMIER SPECTACLE — CONCERT

donné en Février 1920, par Jean Cocteau,

à la Comédie des Champs - Elysées.

I

1. OUVERTURE

Francis Poulenc (première audition)

2. Adieu, New-York!

Fox-trot (première audition)   Georges Auric.
MM. Tommy Foottit & Jackly. *Danse d'acrobates
réglée par Jean Cocteau. Décor et costumes de
Raoul Dufy.*

3. TOUR DE CHANT

KOUBITZKY

Cocardes

Francis Poulenc (première audition)

1. *Miel de Narbonne* — 2. *Bonne d'enfants* —
3. *Enfants de troupe*

Trois chansons populaires avec accompagnement
de petit orchestre, paroles de Jean Cocteau.

Violon: M. Debrun. *Piston:* M. Bailleul. *Trombone:*
M. Mondou. *Grosse caisse:* M. Arnould. *Triangle:*
M. Duhamel.

ENTR'ACTE MUSICAL

BAR

II

1. ORCHESTRE

Erik Satie (première audition)

Trois Petites Pièces Montées

1. *De l'enfance de Pantagruel* (Rêverie)
2. *Marche de Cocagne* (Démarche)
3. *Jeux de Gargantua* (Coin de Polka)

2. Le bœuf sur le toit.

ou THE NOTHING - HAPPENS BAR

Darius Milhaud (première audition). Farce imaginée
et réglée par Jean Cocteau. Costumes de G. P.
Fauconnet. Décor et cartonnages de Raoul Dufy.

La dame décolletée: Albert Fratellini. — *La dame
rousse:* François Fratellini. — *Le barman:* Paul
Fratellini. — *Le policeman:* Bosby. — *Le boxeur
nègre:* Cyrillo. — *Le jockey:* Roberts. — *Le monsieur
en habit:* Pinocchio. — *Nègre qui joue au billard:* Boda.

*Orchestre de 25 musiciens du Théâtre des Champs -
Élysées, dirigé par M. Vladimir Golschmann.*

Costumes exécutés par MUELLE. — Cartonnages moulés par GAYMARD
(Maison Berthelin). — Décors exécutés dans les ateliers de JULES MÉRIOT.

prochain spectacle - concert: festival Erik Satie

Imprimé par François Bernouard.   Prix du programme : DEUX francs.

mention that its venerated managing editor, Galtier Boissière, liked to haunt the more "popular" dives—i. e., resorts of the masses, not of the classes—such as the dark sinister dance halls in the Rue des Vertus, the Rue de Lappe, and the Rue des Gravilliers. It was there that he found a great wealth of ingredients for his gouaches and his series *La Bonne Vie*.

Léger's Ladies

Compared to the subtlety of Cocteau, to the magic of Picasso, or to Kees's ferocity, Fernand Léger's qualities seem rather those of a piano mover. He did not even invent the sort of Machine Age lyricism which his paintings celebrate, but took it over from the pre-1910 Futurists, whose leader was the poet Marinetti, an exuberant Italian somewhat on the Picabia model, but older. Léger's particular "modernism" was a matter of circles and globes and curves drawn as though with a compass. His colors always remained very limited: primary reds, blues, greens, yellows. The paint is put on perfectly flatly, as on the side of a barn.

I am afraid it is at Léger's door we must lay responsibility for all those *Arts Ménagers* (Domestic Science) posters, all those goddesses of industry with wheels inside their heads, symbolizing Reason. His machinery of straight lines and cylinders, so "severe" that even the hair of the heads seems to be made of metal, represents what the larger public was willing to keep of Cubism, the part of Cubism that could be put to commercial use. There was something robot-like about

Serge Lifar.

93

Léger: his painting really can be said to function. It is crankshaft art.

But, by the same token, Léger's painting illustrates the other extreme from Van Dongen's. Léger painted the Ladies of the Twenties the way they liked to think of themselves—shapeless, robot-headed, a moving geometrical pattern, just as Brigitte Helm realized the ideal in the film *Metropolis*. Van Dongen, at the other extreme, painted

Picasso and Stravinsky, by Jean Cocteau.

the Ladies of the Twenties as they really were.

One Ox On All the Roofs of Paris

We have already mentioned *Le Bœuf sur le Toit* several times in these necessarily kaleidoscopic pages. André Fraigneau said it very well. "The Twenties were the Nigger Era, the Jazz Age, the day of the chemise-dress, cropped hair, watered-down Cubism, sexual freedom, gratuitous gestures, meaningless suicides. The golden calf was still around to be worshiped, but nobody talked about it any more. What dominated Paris was an ox on the rooftops."

Le Bœuf sur le Toit may justly be regarded as having been as important a Twenties locale as the sacred triangle at the heart of Montparnasse. It served to crystallize a number of the forces of the age. It was the result of a spontaneous collaboration between talent, wealth, snobbery, and the new informality of manners. Situated in the Rue Boissy-d'Anglas at the peak of its fame, this night club and bar which Jean Cocteau founded (acting at the time as double agent, at once for Olympus and for Paris society), was a godsend to artists, to poets, to musicians, to princesses, to wealthy idlers, and to a few really determined lesbians and gazelle-eyed pederasts—who must at least, these last, be given credit for working with the means at hand, before modern medicine had discovered the miracle of hormones! Basically, the *Bœuf* was Adam's last stand against the roving battalions of Eve. One's only possible criticism might be that the male solidarity there exhibited was a trifle too unilateral!

The history of this establishment—a sort of annex to *Maxim's*—deserves to be carefully related. Its origins go back to a place

The Three Musicians. *Painting by Picasso.*

called *Le Gaya* in the Rue Duphot. The owner of that place was a big burly fellow, a native of the Ardennes, whose name was Moyses. He was having trouble keeping *Le Gaya* filled, and someone suggested he go to see Cocteau, who was then living at 10, Rue d'Anjou. Moyses did so, and remarked on a photograph he saw on Cocteau's wall (in a room very like " the gypsy wagon " in *Les Enfants Terribles*). Moyses recognized the photograph as one of Rimbaud as a child. Jean Oberlé has reconstructed the conversation that followed.

" How strange," Moyses said to Cocteau. " You have the picture of little Arthur."

" You mean, you know who that is a photograph of? " asked Cocteau.

" I certainly ought to. It was in my bedroom in Charleville, where we lived when I was a child."

Cocteau was bowled over. Rimbaud's childhood home—the very house Moyses had lived in—had long played a part in Cocteau's private mythology. He could scarcely refuse to do a favor for someone who came to him in possession of such potent magic.

And so Cocteau took to going to *Le Gaya*, in dinner jacket with red necktie, and an opera hat. He would sit in at the drums with Auric and Milhaud. Jean Wiener was the pianist. The place quickly caught on, and before long the premises were much too small. Then Moyses moved to the Rue Boissy-d'Anglas. In the meantime, Paris had acquired a new center, not of gravity, but of its opposite.

Take, for example, the list of patronesses

" Chic requires nothing at all. It is much more the way you carry your head than the way you wear your clothes."

for one of the Comte de Beaumont's famous and ultra-fashionable *soirées de Paris*, this one held not at *Le Bœuf* but at *La Cigale*. Étienne de Beaumont's affairs were charity balls for such causes as war widows and Russian refugees, and were conceived in conjunction

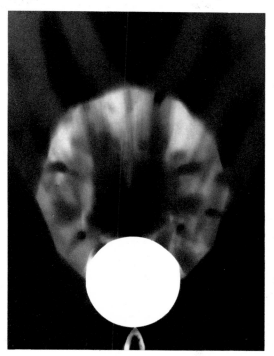

Rayogram by Man Ray. (Film exposed directly to light, not through lens.)

with the season of the Ballets Russes, throughout their declining years. For one of them, the following great ladies served : the Duchesse d'Audiffret-Pasquier, Princesse Philippe de Caraman-Chimay, Princesse Lucien Murat, the Duchesse, Marquise, and Comtesse de Noailles, the Duchesse de Rohan, and the always lovely Missia Sert... It was the Vicomtesse de Japy who made the appropriate remark, after her husband's death: " Paris is becoming deforested."

The aristocracy, persons from the middle-class of business and finance, Cocteau and the

Perfume Bottle designed by Paul Iribe.

new musicians, even the Faubourg Saint-Germain—all met and mingled at the *Bœuf* sur le Toit. Maurice Sachs said later: " It was the place where our true masters were present."

For " society " had survived from the last century. There were in the Twenties such figures as Prince Jean-Louis de Faucigny-Lucinge, the Comte de Fels, Captain Molyneux (who founded the great dressmaking house), Prince Georges Ghika, Comte Stanislas de la Rochefoucauld, the Vicomte de Noailles (who financed the films made by Buñuel and Dali, including the scandalous *L'Age d'Or*, and Cocteau's *Blood of a Poet*), the Barons de Rothschild, the Comte de Lesseps, and the Princesse de Polignac, patroness of modern music...

" At the *Bœuf*," noted Maurice Sachs (who never picked up the check at his table, we may be sure), " everyone wears an expression of amazement." Radiguet went there, by no means happy to be treated as a *Wunderkind*. Blaise Cendrars, also—on Christmas Eve of 1925 he brought his dog with him. Paul Morand, Erik Satie (dean of modern music, always in cutaway, with bowler hat and umbrella), Max Jacob wearing his monocle, Christian Bérard as yet unbearded (but already unkempt), Gérard Bauer planning to launch the first summer season along the Riviera, the lovely Mme Letellier, wife of the editor of the *Journal*, Mme Georges Menier, René Clair, King Ferdinand of Roumania... Cariatys, not as yet married to Marcel Jouhandeau, may do one of her dances for us, and perhaps Marcel Herrand will sing. Jacques Doucet and Jean Wiener take turns at the piano,

Kandinsky's cosmic structures were not appreciated in the Twenties. Thirty years have had to go by, about the right distance in time to keep between the literary photographer and his subject.

improvising irreverent variations on Chopin. Chopinata ! Between numbers, Doucet may be caught reading a detective story.

Kiki

For a while it seemed that Paris—the " Paris, she-is-a-Woman " city—had at last appeared in the flesh. For a while Paris *was* Kiki of Montparnasse, the poor but beautiful model who while still quite small was haunting café terraces in search of a café-crème, and who could have been seen sitting between Modigliani and Soutine as early as 1918, at Ludion's.

In 1920, Alice Prin, who was never called anything but Kiki, made the rounds of the cafés selling the magazine *Montparnasse*. She made five sous (25 centimes) on each copy she sold, and at that time a café-crème cost only ten sous. So life was perfect. When she needed a bath, she would make a pal of the woman who supervised the toilets, and clean up there. She always had a pleasant smile, and her repertory of songs would have made a top sergeant blush. She became the painter Kisling's *amie*, and has herself described how she became acquainted with the man, in whom the character of an Eastern potentate mingled with that of a street Arab.

" One day I noticed a new customer at the *Rotonde*. He was deeply tanned by the sun and wore his hair with a sort of fringe across the forehead. I decided he was rather a nasty bit of goods and tried not to let him see me looking at him. I heard him ask the manager, ' Who's the new whore? ' That didn't make me like him any better. A man I knew told me, ' That's Kisling. I'll introduce you.' After that, whenever he saw me around one of the cafés, even from a distance, he would call out to me, using the most awful language. He would even call me a codfish, sometimes... It was too bad, because I liked him. Then one day he promised he wouldn't yell at me like that anymore. He gave me a three-month contract."

Canvases presenting Kiki in one or another pose, invariably nude, were piling up all through the Twenties in Montparnasse studios. Today they are scattered throughout museums all over the world.

" I knew one other painter who was as much fun as Kisling. It was Foujita. In that funny accent of his, he used to ask me, ' Why you feet dirty? '—not being able to pronounce *r*. In those days I nearly always went around barefoot. Foujita used to like me to sing *Louise* for him. I would imitate the orchestra, and I even had a little flute solo worked in. It always made him laugh and laugh. ' C'est *igolo*,' he'd say, ' *C'est igolo !* ' " (For *rigolo*, " funny.")

Like Colette's Claudine, but one who had been educated in the wrong schools, Kiki had a little cupid's-bow mouth, eyes the color of *marc de Bourgogne*, and a camellia-like complexion. She was never seen with anyone but painters and poets. When she sang, she sang with her whole body, which was a very beautiful one. Unlike many women of the period, she was not ashamed of her breasts.

Kiki was Queen of Montparnasse. In those days, not all the Americans there were non-professionals. Some were practicing artists. One of them, Man Ray, was crazy about Kiki. Photographing her one day in the nude, he said, " Kiki, stop looking at me like that ! You bother me ! "

His photographs of her are extraordinary. I have it on the authority of Florent Fels, author of *L'Art et l'Amour* and editor-in-chief of *L'Art Vivant*, that Man Ray invented an automatic shutter so that he could take photographs of Kiki and himself in their more intimate moments.

Montparnasse went right on growing, with a new cabaret opening every week or so. When Kiki was singing at the *Jockey*, you would be sure to see Kisling, Zborowsky, Fels, and the Rag Doll *(La Môme Chiffon)* who went around the tables begging.

One thing is clear now, when we go back in memory to these times. The purpose of the dance was to feel giddy. Paris was getting bored. As they became successful, the painters moved away from Montparnasse. Picasso went to live in the Rue La Boétie. After Modigliani died, Utrillo never went back to Montparnasse... Elsewhere in Paris, Cocteau was preoccupied with his *Antigone*. Certain of them became more and more caught up in Communism, especially Picasso, Eluard, and Aragon. The newer painters were going in for Freudian *trompe-l'œil*, or turning toward abstraction. André Breton was beginning his long search for wisdom among the ancient Celts, the occultists, and the forgotten moderns. Foujita moved into lavish quarters and kept a garage full of elaborately nickel-plated automobiles, rivaled only by Picabia's and the car that Braque designed for Cendrars.

Youki, or Pink Snow

She arrived in Paris in 1921, a blonde from the Walloon region of Belgium (Pepinster, near Liège), intending to go into the movies. She was willowy thin, with great wide eyes and rounded cheekbones. Her name was Lucie. One day she happened to read the book by Apollinaire, *La Femme Assise*, in which he spoke of Montparnasse, and from that moment on, nothing else mattered.

Lucie was a really pretty new face. She fell in love with Foujita at the *Rotonde*, and became his wife. She saw him as a kind of Buddha, while he baptized her Youki, which means " pink snow " in Japanese. He painted an enormous nude of her, which was hung in the 1924 *Salon d'Automne*. (For a long time now, the other *Salons* had ceased to count; there were only the *Automne* and the *Indépendants*.) Picasso went to the opening and stopped in front of the picture. It was titled " Youki, Goddess of Snow." Picasso spoke to Foujita, pointing to Youki herself, who was also standing there. " She is even more beautiful than your picture."

This Flemish beauty may be considered representative of all the lovely girls who lived with painters during this period. She liked to go dancing at *La Boule Noire* and *Le Bal Nègre* in the Rue Blomet. At a time when Paul Colin's Negro saxophonists were still a novelty, such places had a genuinely exotic appeal, but they also served as expression for another phase of the Twenties' sexual freedom. It was now considered perfectly proper for Eve to dance with colored men, and there was nothing to object to if a white woman and a Negro man, or a Negro woman and a white man, fell in love.

Sometime during 1925, Youki Foujita was in a little bar in the Rue Bréa one afternoon. (It is today known as the *O. K. Bar*.) She noticed a tall, thin young man with straight hair plastered down, and heavy glasses. His name was Robert Desnos, and he was doing things with the paper that drinking straws are wrapped in. " He was twisting the bits of paper into the shape of spiders," Youki

101

relates. "He would then put a tiny drop of his drink in the middle of them, and they would begin to move."

"Do you know this game?" Desnos inquired.

"Of course, I do," Youki replied. "It's one of those Surrealist games."

Now, although the Surrealists were not—not any of them—Montparnos, preferring mostly the *Certa* bar, or the Rue Fontaine, everybody knew about everybody else in those days. Youki was surprised to hear this tall young man, who looked more like a bank clerk than a poet, say "Well, yes—but I'm the one who showed them how." Which may have been true, so far as this particular game is concerned.

Youki found Desnos quite dull at first. A few days later she ran into him again at the bar of the *Coupole*, where the bartender's name was Bob. "I was struck by the oyster color of his eyes, and the dark circles under them," Youki tells us. "He had a nice big mouth and smiled very pleasantly."

"You have magnificent eyes, Desnos. At bottom you're probably not so impossible as you seemed the other afternoon."

"But I'm very nice!" Desnos protested, without a trace of affectation.

Conversations like these between men and women in the Twenties must startle a few persons today. Youki, in any case, felt obliged to explain things a bit more, when she wrote her reminiscences.

"The kind of life we led in those days was not peculiar, in terms of the general atmosphere. It wasn't just the artists who lived like that. Nights we would wander back and forth from Montparnasse to Montmartre, maybe stopping off somewhere in the Champs-Élysées. All the movement was leisurely, and yet at the same time there was an inner excitement about it—I can only compare it to the movement of a Cartesian diver, or to the specks of gold in a bottle of Danzig brandy when you shake it... Let's say I'm sitting at the *Dôme*. There I might run into Pascin, Lucy Krogh, Hermine David. That would be in one wave of arrivals. Then on the next wave would come in Soutine, Kisling, Basler, Robert Desnos, Jacques Prévert... Then I'd get up to go, and move along to the *Coupole*, where I would see Antonin Artaud, perhaps, or Pierre Brasseur, Solange Sicard, or Fernande Barrey... Then after a while it would be time to go on to the *Select*, where there would be still another company, or perhaps some of the ones you had already run into at the *Dôme*."

This passage from *Confidences de Youki* describes very well the choreographic pattern followed—it would seem, instinctively—by the night wanderers of the Twenties. Can't you hear the orchestra playing—playing, indeed, until you can't stand to hear another note of it—*Je cherche après Titine?*

As Time Goes By

The texture of an age is made up of hundreds of tiny events. The revival of *Phi-Phi* makes us able to listen better to *La Belle Hélène*. The blind composer René de Buxeuil remained faithful to an image of womankind which, to tell the truth, never really disappeared save in "smart" circles:

> They have a soul, the roses,
> For they are women, roses.

The housing problem grew steadily worse. Servants were increasingly hard to find and keep. A society accustomed to luxury had never before had such trouble *getting waited on.* Although still shaped like speaking tubes or hunting horns, telephones had become a necessity in daily life, while in the theater they were as ubiquitous in a Sacha Guitry boulevard comedy as in an avant-garde play by Cocteau. The radio was only just making its appearance—quite nakedly exposing its innards for all to marvel at.

There had been some changes in the popular idea of how the man who is irresistible to women should look. Men's hats were broader of brim, and choice shades of felt were " nigger brown " and " prairie green." Maurice Chevalier's straw boater was not recognized as a throwback to the Nineties. The masses remained faithful to the man's cap, with and without visor, but the so-called " three-decker " Apache cap was a thing of the past. Men's wear manufacturers declared war on the nightgown and the shirt-tail. What, now, will the actors in burlesque blackout skits do, as they dash out of bed and run for the closet at the husband's unexpected return? In smart circles the pyjama was already solving this problem. You had your choice of the Mandarin style, or the " Tiger Skin."

Camille Flammarion, portly and bearded, had all of France hanging on his words as he lectured on the planet Mars. It was good manners, when you were at the wheel of your 40 h. p. Renault and not driving too fast, to raise your hat to acquaintances. The Seznec scandal ran its course, and the body of Jean Jaurès was translated to the Panthéon. Deauville, whose social arbiter was a stickler for protocol and ceremony (an attitude, it was rumored, that could be explained by his origins and manner of advancement in the world), was now a suburb of Paris. Along the boardwalk it was customary to recognize the Indian maharajah in the red bathing suit, the Chicago multimillionnaire in the old brown sweater, the good-looking scoundrel who fleeces women, and the film goddess. One evening the Casino took in 835,000 francs (which would come to over 40 million today). Men and women in evening clothes now danced right out on the water.

The discovery of King Tut's tomb was news of stop-press order. *L'Illustration* had a special number, supplying a reading glass to help the reader decipher the hieroglyphics. Cécile Sorel had her picture taken in front of the Sphinx—the one in Egypt, that is. The one in Paris remained open, meanwhile.

Rip was appearing in *Le Tracassin* at the Potinière. There was a campaign to do away with the cane. " This campaign will never succeed. The cane is to the hands what the smile is to the lips." While the great preacher Father Sanson was packing them in at Notre-Dame, the Gertrude Hoffman Girls were packing them in at the Music-Hall des Champs-Élysées.

When General de Castelnau addressed 50,000 members of the Ligue Catholique, a little black box was held up in front of his lips and his words were piped from it to two old gramophone speakers at either side of the platform. The age of the rally, of the mass-meeting, had dawned. Blood transfusions were now quite common; they were considered rather unpleasant to think about, but obviously of great practical value. In 1926 Stravinsky recorded his *Fire Bird*, and it was reported that " The illusion of the orchestra is perfect," but that there was still some scratching. The Louvre hung Seurat's *Le Cirque*. At the Atelier, the actor-manager Charles Dullin ordered the tipping of ushers to stop. The resulting outcry suggested he had endangered public morals. Jacques Coupeau, disappointed with Paris, went off to evangelize the provinces. At his theater, the Pitoëffs took over. The leading playwrights were Marcel Achard, Jacques Deval, Henri Bernstein, Marcel Pagnol, Jules Romains, Luigi Pirandello, and Cocteau. Jacques Hébertot took over the management of the Théâtre des Champs-Élysées, where the Swedish Ballets of Rolf de Maré would shortly open with the memorable dancer Jean Borlin. The memory of the Ballets Russes had not, however, disappeared. In the novel, the M's now took over: Morand, Mauriac, Malraux, Montherlant, and Mac Orlan. They replaced the B's: Bourget, Bazin, Bordeaux, etc.

In 1926 the Douanier Rousseau's *The Sleeping Gypsy* brought a price of 525,000 francs at the Hôtel des Ventes; whether it was the transaction or the picture that was hissed and booed is not clear. The French Government paid 95,000 francs (it would come to nearly 5 millions of today's money) for Van Dongen's portrait of Anatole France. Only five years before, it had been considered a scandalous painting.

It was the heyday of the Style Gomina. Architecture was becoming more and more bare and functional. In home furnishings, the reign of Dufayel was closing, finished off by Sauvage, Ruhlmann, and Dufresne. Paul Colin's advertising posters reflected the mounting interest in aviation and transformed the appearance of streets and subway boardings. Léger's robot finally replaced Capiello's little ladies.

Théodore Botrel, the living harp, went to his reward. Aristide Bruant followed shortly afterwards, far less appreciated than he is today. It was the vaudeville theaters that drove out the old *caf' conc'*, where you sat with a mint syrup and seltzer in front of you and watched the performers. The vaudeville theaters were themselves becoming livelier, offering more and better paced shows, with such performers as the great Damia (the Phèdre of the gutters), Colleano, Pomiès, the Fratellini, Raquel Meller, Barbette (the ambiguous acrobat), Mistinguett and Chevalier (both together and apart). In the all-colored revue at the Champs-Élysées, little Florence Mills, the star, suddenly died. Her place was taken by a newcomer whose name was Joséphine Baker. At the saxophone in the orchestra was one Sidney Bechet, of whom nobody had ever heard.

In April, 1927, Nungesser and Coli took off and never returned. Oddly, on the fuselage of their plane there had been painted a death's head, with crossed bones, and a candlestick on either side.

In 1929 the death of Serge de Diaghilev was reported from Venice. One more black gondola crossed the lagoons to the cemetery. The curtain went down forever on the Ballets Russes. All that could complete the débâcle would be if the ox were to come down off the roof.

The Last Party

The last large-scale celebration in Paris before the post-war ended (and began to become the pre-war) was the *Fête Ubu*, a party named in honor of Alfred Jarry's monstrous farce hero, and given by Madeleine Anspach at the *Bal Nègre* in the Rue Blomet. Youki came as a Queen, with a long train and her long blond hair in braids. Kiki led off the dancing, tireless and as uninhibited as ever. Foujita came dressed as a licensed streetwalker. This was in the spring of 1929. And it was actually called the *Fête Ubu!* Nobody, attempting to discover the symbolic significance of the affair, could possibly do better !

The franc had been falling ever since the mid-Twenties. Maurice Sachs, the diabolic chronicler of the Twenties in general and the *Bœuf sur le Toit* in particular—whose life was to end with a fantastic disappearance in Germany during the Second World War—made the following entry in his diary sometime during 1926 : " Were it not for a minister like Poincaré, the inflation here would be as bad as in Germany. The pound sterling is up to 240. Foreigners are pouring into Paris. The signs of prosperity all about are just whistlings in the dark."

Somewhat later, on October 30, 1929, he made another entry: " Yesterday there was a frightful, monstrous financial crash in Wall Street. My uncle, Richard E. Wallason, committed suicide. We are completely wiped out. I'm not going to have the time to keep this diary much longer."

The party was over. Now it was necessary to go to work. After the Wall Street crash, nobody could fool himself any longer about the nature of the Twenties' prosperity. The curtain came down. Madeleine Anspach committed suicide in Liège.

Plea for a " Decadent " Age

It was to the music of Offenbach that the age of the Second Empire, led by Napoleon III, danced its way to the defeat of Sedan. The Cubist society of the Twenties discovered that the music of the Charleston served much the same function, in the end. Any tune can serve for a *danse macabre*.

Also, no period situated between epochs of war and disaster comes off very well at the hands of the historian. Necessarily, it appears frivolous, perhaps even in bad taste. Audiences are sometimes shocked today by the hilarious runaway hearse in René Clair's *Entr'acte*, and the bit where the mourners, lacking a corpse, become restless and start picking and eating at the funeral wreaths. Any epoch that was not a great epoch always has faults in the eyes of its descendants.

However, let us examine the matter more closely. Just as there were (only a year or so ago) *two* Existentialisms, one of great philosophical seriousness and the other consisting of bobby-soxers and blues singers, so there was a Twenties of enduring merit as well as one of ephemeral fun and games. It is particularly important to grasp this before the Twenties become as universally fashionable as the Nineties before them—before, that is, everyone has decided they simply *must* have one of those (atrocious) smoking stands, vintage 1925.

For all the Twenties' failure to increase the national population, it was extremely fertile in other ways. It is doubtful, for example, that anything really new has been done in any of the arts since Cubism, Fauvism, Surrealism, and Abstract Art were launched. The museums of five continents pay tribute to all that was conceived within the small areas extending between the Rue Ravignan and the big galleries—on the one side of the Seine—and in those two other (still smaller) locales: the triangle at the heart of Montparnasse, and the *Bœuf sur le Toit*. Our own day is much more intellectual-reflective in mood, much less creative in the arts. Between the Impressionists of the late nineteenth century and the close of the Twenties, French painting—that is, a School of Paris, greatly supported by talents drawn from abroad—enjoyed a period of world greatness comparable to the great epochs of Venice and Antwerp.

If the other arts have had less enormous an influence than painting, it still must not be forgotten that Dada is the direct precursor of present-day philosophies " of the absurd "; that the influence of Surrealism in literature has been worldwide; and that with *Les Six*, French music produced a modern school in every sense comparable to those of other nations. It is Le Corbusier who has been commissioned to plan and build cities on the other side of the world!

Nor, in the realm of ideas, was serious discussion ever livelier than it was in the Twenties. A Renaissance taste for intellectual matters, as expressed in controversies ranging from that over Pure Poetry to that over Disarmament, produced lasting results, as well as stimulated curiosity. Valéry's marmoreal pessimism, Gide's contagious frankness, Claudel's great overblown epic poems and plays, Mauriac's curious blend of musical utterance with venomous sense, none of this has been forgotten or ceased to be influential. Maritain's revival of Thomism must be cited, as must also the advance of psychoanalytical research and therapy. Nor should we forget the adventuresomeness and talent of French publishers in the Twenties, especially honoring the names of Grasset and the *Nouvelle Revue Française*.

What remains, after surveying the period in some detail, is a sense of its appetite for life, for light and movement. Florent Fels described it in this way: " Between 1920 and 1930 nobody doubted but that he was on the way to creating something; we were not out to change the world, but we were trying to make it look different and think differently."

And so we come to the question of manners and morals. Such a naughty age! It is curious to note today the severity with which many survivors of the Twenties, men and women alike, rail at the young for their " Existentialist-style " behavior: the cellar clubs, the interracial dances, the casual relations between the sexes. It is necessary to have a very short memory indeed, not to be amused when contemporaries of Colette—that great artist and unequivocally " loose " woman—or of Radiguet, men and women who themselves danced *La Jazzbandette*, reproach Françoise Sagan for the *immoral* behavior of her characters! We are even told they are shocked by her automobile accident! One can only remind them of all they have forgotten, from the nocturnal gambols in the Bois de Boulogne to the *Fête Ubu...*

It is quite true that Paris in the Twenties was dissolute, immoral, and that the birth rate dropped. Perversions were openly discussed and, sometimes, openly practiced. If we are no more virtuous today, at least we are quieter! And it could be argued that the cause of " sexual liberation " was not worth all the attention it got. Fewer people today are being " converted " to fewer causes. Which is a good thing. The epidemic of suicides has passed, the result of a world spinning too wildly on its axis. And finally, if the modern woman has continued her pursuit of equality, she has more often directed her energies into politics and her work. There is nothing to regret in the fact that the Twenties attempt to restore the matriarchy did not succeed.

Paris in the Twenties was more head than heart. This, I think, is the worst we can say of it. It was far from being "socially conscious." It went to extremes, to excess. Although we are probably not in a position to reproach the Twenties for their homosexuality, what is there to say about all the lovemaking in public, all the drinking, and the drugging? Paris in the Twenties was intoxicated with the possession of personal, private liberty, and it did not always observe Cocteau's injunction to the effect that one must know just how far to go too far.

As for ourselves, living in an era of crushing conformities of many varieties, conscious of how many publications, drawings, and other work of the Twenties can no longer be reprinted or reproduced, and somewhat puzzled as to the real foundations of this new and highly moral order, it is impossible to look back on the Twenties without nostalgia.

This decade of our history remains stunning in its audacity, its Bohemianism, its outspokenness, its bad manners, and its creative power. We may even, in an epoch of national decline, speak of its greatness. Jules Romains spoke with his usual promptness—in Montparnasse, in the Twenties—when he summed it all up: A time and a place without peer or parallel.

A moment of time forever lost.

Armand Lanoux

CREDITS

7 Gazette du Bon Ton. / 8. 9. 11 Photos Monde et Caméra. / 12 Photo Harlingue.

13 Dr. Roudinesco Collection. Paris. Color photo Facchetti. / 14. 15 Photos Lartigue.

16 Gazette du Bon Ton. / 17 Photo Harlingue. / 20 Photo Lartigue.

23 Document Sirot. / 24. 25 Anatole Jakovsky Collection. Paris.

27 Georges Besson Collection. Paris. Color photo Laniepce. / 28 Document Romi.

31 Musée du Petit Palais. Paris. Color photo Giraudon. / 32 Photo Man Ray.

35 Dr. Roudinesco Collection. Paris. Color photo Facchetti. / 36 Document Romi.

37. 38. 39. 40 Photos Monde et Caméra. / 41. 42 Photos Lartigue.

44 Gabriel Clayeux Collection. Paris. / 45 Photo Lipnitzki.

48 Fan from Paquin. Michel de Brunhoff Collection. Paris.

49 Document Romi. / 50 Photo Lartigue. / 52. 53 Documents Romi.

54 Marcel l'Herbier Collection. Paris. / 57 Gazette du Bon Ton.

58 Tristan Tzara Collection. Paris. Photo Man Ray.

60 Henri Sauguet Collection. Paris. Photo Schall. / 61 Gazette du Bon Ton.

62 Photo Bibliothèque Nationale. Paris. / 63 Photo Monde et Caméra. / 64 Photo Lipnitzki.

65 Gazette du Bon Ton. / 66 Michel de Brunhoff Collection. Paris.

69 Moltzau Collection. Stockholm. Color photo Conzett et Huber.

70 Anatole Jakovsky Collection. Paris. / 71 Photo Lartigue.

72 Dr. Roudinesco Collection. Paris. Photo Facchetti. / 75 Photo Lartigue.

76 Document Max, Furrier in Paris.

77 Moltzau Collection. Stockholm. Color photo Conzett et Huber. / 78 Document Romi.

81 Roland Penrose Collection. London. Color photo Fleming. / 82 Photo Isabey.

83. 85 Tristan Tzara Collection. Paris. / 84 Tristan Tzara Collection. Paris. Photo Man Ray.

86 Berggruen Collection. Paris. Photo Cauvin. / 87 Photo Lipnitzki. / 88 Document Romi.

90. 92 Henri Sauguet Collection. Paris. / 93 Photo Lipnitzki.

94 Museum of Modern Art Collection. New York. Mrs. Simon Guggenheim Fund. Color photo.

Museum of Modern Art. / 97 Photo Man Ray. / 98 Michel de Brunhoff Collection. Paris.

99 Seidler Collection. Munich. Color photo Hinz.

The publisher would like to thank the museum curators and private collectors for their generous assistance in assembling this book. Especial thanks are due Messrs. Michel de Brunhoff, Georges Lepape, Romi, Dr. Roudinesco, Henri Sauguet, and Tristan Tzara.

This book was designed and edited by Robert Delpire and Jacques Monory. Printed by Draeger Frères, Montrouge (France).